• HALSGROVE DISCOVER SERIES ➤

JANE AUSTEN AND BATH

TERRY TOWNSEND

HALSGROVE

First published in Great Britain in 2015

Copyright © Terry Townsend 2015

All rights reserved. No part of this publication may be
reproduced, stored in a retrieval system, or transmitted
in any form or by any means without the prior permission
of the copyright holder.

British Library Cataloguing-in-Publication Data
A CIP record for this title is available from the British Library

ISBN 978 0 85704 254 5

HALSGROVE
Halsgrove House, Ryelands Business Park,
Bagley Road, Wellington, Somerset TA21 9PZ
Tel: 01823 653777   Fax: 01823 216796
email: sales@halsgrove.com

Part of the Halsgrove group of companies.
Information on all Halsgrove titles is
available at: www.halsgrove.com

Printed in China by Everbest Printing Co Ltd

Acknowledgements

I would particularly like to thank
Adrienne Bradney-Smith for generously sharing her knowledge
and advising on the manuscript as a whole.
Also Brenda and Tony Stables and Deirdre Le Faye
for their encouragement and editorial help.

Thanks to Martyn Folkes of Mushroom Publishing
156 Southlands, Bath, BA1 4EB, United Kingdom
for permission to include the Bath City Centre Street Map.

Selected Bibliography

Northanger Abbey	Jane Austen
Persuasion	Jane Austen
The Georgian Buildings of Bath	Walter Ison
A Charming Place – Bath in the Life & Novels of Jane Austen	Maggie Lane
Jane Austen & Regency Bath	Maggie Lane
Jane Austen's Letters – Collected & Edited	Deirdre Le Faye
The World of Jane Austen	Nigel Nicolson
Bath as Jane Austen Knew It (Part 1 & Part 2)	Terry Old
Jane Austen in Bath	Katharine Reeve
Literary Walks in Bath	Andrew Swift and Kirsten Elliott
On Foot in Bath	Andrew Swift

To Carol
collaborator and friend

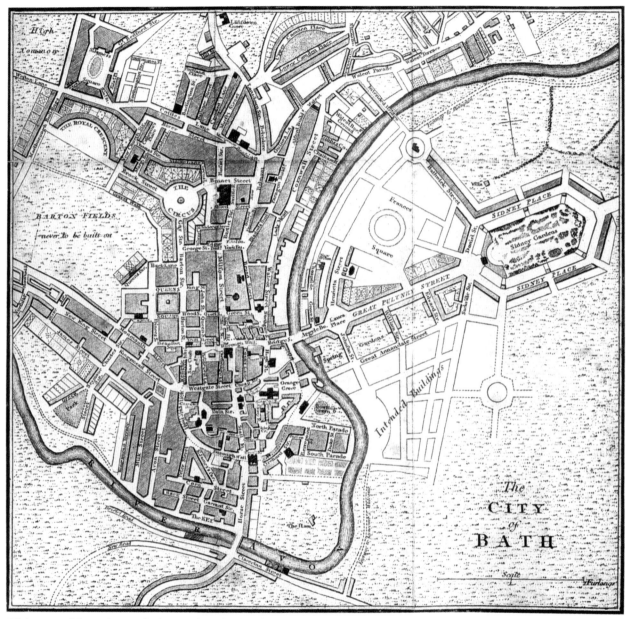

This map of Georgian Bath shows plans for developments on the Pulteney Estate which were never completed. It also shows a section of Green Park Buildings which was destroyed in the bombing of 1942.

Contents

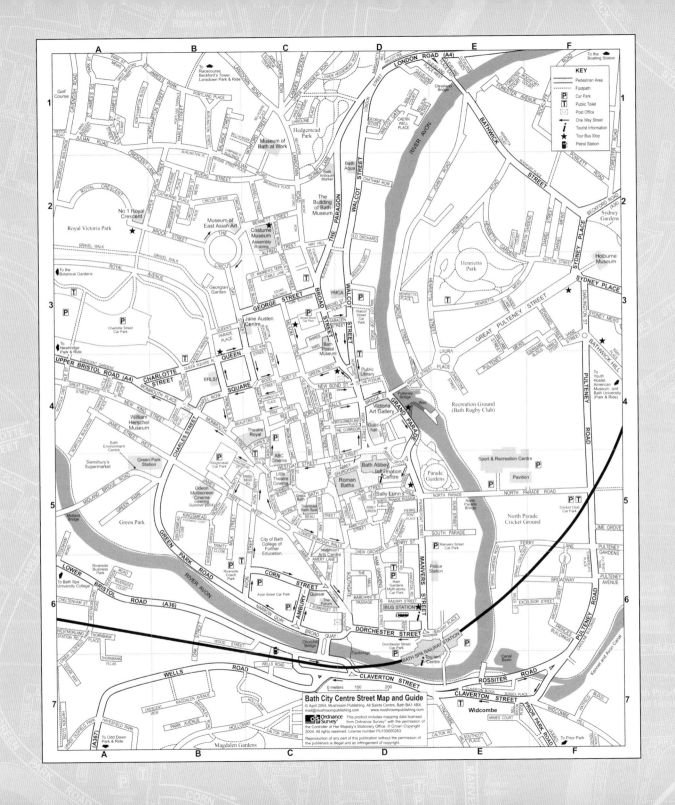

Bath City Centre Street Map and Guide

© April 2004, Mushroom Publishing, All Saints Centre, Bath BA1 4BX.
mail@mushroompublishing.com   www.mushroompublishing.com

Foreword

Bath is unique. There is no other town in England where one can get closer to the eighteenth-century experience. The streets of tall, pale, seemingly identical houses, ranged in terraces or curving crescents, create a rhythmic harmony which never ceases to delight the eye. What's more, to stroll around these graceful streets and squares is to walk in the steps of Jane Austen.

Although Jane's characters are precisely drawn, the settings in her novels are often tantalisingly vague. In *Pride and Prejudice*, she is careful to keep the actual location of the Hertfordshire town of Meryton a secret. Enthusiasts continue to search in vain for *Emma's* Surrey village of Highbury. The exception to this coy approach is Bath.

References to Bath occur from time to time throughout all six novels. Moreover Jane was confident enough in her knowledge of its heart and environs to make Bath the main setting for two of them; *Northanger Abbey* and *Persuasion*. Such is the continued appeal of these romances they have become a major factor in the reason why people from around the world are drawn to the city.

In addition to the novels there is another resource which provides an insight into the time Jane spent in Bath. These are the letters she wrote to Cassandra when the two sisters were apart. From these sources a detailed picture emerges of public buildings such as the pump room and the baths where invalids sought solace from their ills; and the assembly rooms, shops and theatres which were a magnet for Georgian pleasure-seekers.

Opposite: *The present day map makes an interesting comparison, with the city as Jane knew it.*

Each text entry in the guide has a key e.g. Queen Square [map B4].

The romance of the two Bath novels has an enduring appeal.

9

Jane Austen's legacy continues to attract visitors from around the world.

Jane Austen's writing is so fresh and immediate, it allows us to feel a direct connection with her experience.

Opposite: The architectural harmony of Bath's elegant terraces and curving crescents never ceases to delight the eye.

Right: The grand assembly rooms frequented by Jane and her characters can still be visited.

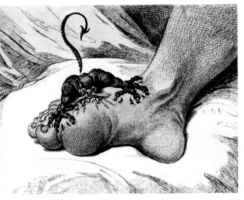

The agony and the irony. This ugly 1799 caricature by James Gilray graphically conveys the misery of gout. Ironically the beautiful city of Bath was largely founded on people being drawn to the spa seeking relief from this ailment known as 'the rich mans' condition'.

More intimately we learn of private houses where she holidayed or lived for periods with her family and the houses of her friends where she was invited for afternoon tea or evening card parties. She carefully selected houses like these as lodgings for her characters, whose rank and status she conveyed simply by their addresses, a code her readers at the time readily understood.

Jane Austen's legacy is such that we can look at a stylish house in one of the crescents and easily imagine a carriage sporting a baronet's crest drawing up in front. Torch snuffers, still in place by some of the doorways, are redolent of the time 'link boys' with flaming torches led the way at night for sedan chair carriers. With a little imagination we might envisage a chair being set down and a fashionable lady alighting to enter elegant rooms softly lit with candles and the glint of silver.

At almost every corner or flight of steps, at every narrow court or wide promenade, and even in outlying villages there are associations to be found with Jane Austen. Although more than two centuries have passed, her writing remains so fresh and immediate it allows us to feel a direct connection with her world.

Right: Link snuffers remain an evocative feature on a number of houses.

Far right: With a little imagination we might envisage a sedan chair being set down allowing for a fashionable lady to alight.

Introduction

Jane Austen's experience of Bath, as a visitor and resident, spans at least eight years from 1797 and there are hints of possible earlier visits. However, the depth of her family connections with the Georgian city and its heritage extend over the whole eighty years of its development, from the time the first stone was laid.

The story essentially concerns three individual relatives, all from her mother's side and each separated by a generation. They are James Brydges, Theophilus Leigh and James Leigh-Perrot, all with health problems and all drawn to Bath by the medicinal qualities attributed to the spa waters.

Jane's mother was a great-niece of millionaire entrepreneur James Brydges, first Duke of Chandos. The duke was obviously suffering stress when he first visited Bath in the early 1700s seeking a cure for his 'twitching nerves' and 'hysterical fits'.

At that time, except for sections of the city walls, all traces of the Roman town had disappeared. The medieval settlement James Brydges encountered was ramshackle and dirty. Available accommodation for the wealthy of his class was woefully inadequate and he saw an investment opportunity.

Working through an agent he purchased a parcel of land, in a confidential deal, which was part of the old St John's Hospital. Discreet enquiries for a competent stonemason produced twenty-two-year-old John Wood who at the time was working on a low-paid project intended to make the River Avon navigable from Bath to Bristol.

Wood entered into a contract with James Brydges on 23 January 1727. The direct result of this collaboration was 'Chandos Buildings' and the adjacent development of the St John's Hospital complex; both standing just within the city walls facing west across open countryside.

Jane's illustrious ancestor, James Brydges, first Duke of Chandos, was the pioneer of Georgian Bath's property developers.

Chandos Buildings funded by James Brydges and built by architect John Wood.

St John's Hospital and the adjacent Chandos Buildings stood just within the old city wall facing open countryside.

This was the first of John Wood's considerable architectural achievements in Bath but the level of investment return was less than Brydges expected and he withdrew from any further property speculation. However his employment of John Wood became the dramatic catalyst for future city development.

Other entrepreneurs were encouraged to fund projects and soon the enterprising Wood was sufficiently established to begin speculative building projects of his own. From this early beginning the far-sighted Wood went on to create Queen Square, North and South Parades and the spectacular King's Circus. His son, John Wood the Younger, following his father's lead, extended the city well beyond the old boundary walls and created his own masterpiece, the Royal Crescent.

* * *

Theophilus Leigh, Jane's great uncle was Master of Balliol College, Oxford for more than fifty years.

Long before James Brydges became involved in Bath property development, his sister Mary had married Theophilus Leigh of Adlestrop in Gloucestershire. Mary and Theophilus had twelve children, two of whom were significant in the Jane Austen story. The first, also named Theophilus, became Master of Balliol College, Oxford where he remained for more than half a century. While living in Bath Jane's mother Cassandra Leigh visited her uncle Theophilus in Oxford and it is thought she met the Rev'd George Austen at that time.

Jane Austen's maternal grandfather, Thomas Leigh, another son of Theophilus Leigh and Mary Brydges, became Rector of Harpsden in Oxfordshire. By the time of his retirement from the church he was severely afflicted with gout. Thomas settled in Bath with his wife Jane (née Perrot) and son James together with his two unmarried daughters Jane and Cassandra. Cassandra Leigh was to become Jane Austen's mother.

In October 1764, Thomas's son James Leigh married the twenty-year-old Jane Cholmeley. When James inherited estates at Northleigh in Oxfordshire from the Perrot family he added their name to his own, becoming James Leigh-Perrot. The first record of Jane Austen visiting Bath came about as the result of an invitation from the Leigh-Perrots to stay with them at their home in the Paragon.

* * *

In a sense, Jane Austen's personal story began in Bath at St Swithin's church in the parish of Walcot on 26 April 1764, when her mother Cassandra Leigh married the Rev'd George Austen. Cassandra was a resident of Bath and St Swithin's was her parish church.

Part of George and Cassandra's courtship would have taken place in Bath during the time when it was second only to London for entertainment and gaiety. There were opportunities for parties, theatre going and dances held in the Assembly Rooms. Although her stay in Bath was short it must have been an exciting time for Cassandra Leigh, who had spent her formative years in the quiet rectory in Harpsden near Henley-on-Thames.

On their wedding day George and Cassandra left Bath to begin their married life in Hampshire. Rev'd George Austen had been appointed to the living of Steventon, a small village in the north of the county. Eleven years later, on 16 December 1775, Jane was born, the seventh of their eight children. The only other girl, born almost three years before Jane, was given the family Christian name of Cassandra.

Top: *The Rev'd George Austen, Jane's father.*

Above: *Cassandra Austen née Leigh, Jane's mother.*

Left: *Walcot church, Bath where Jane's parents were married on 26 April 1764 was replaced in 1777 by the present-day building.*

17

During Jane's formative years in the quiet country neighbourhood, there must have been much discussion about Bath and Jane would have formed an impression of the city well before she came to experience it first-hand.

*   *   *

In 1797 Mrs Austen took her two daughters for a holiday in Bath staying with her brother James Leigh-Perrot and his wife. During the period she had been absent from the city, many more people could afford to travel and take holidays. She must have been amazed by the city's growth, the number of houses having increased by a massive forty-five percent.

The main new developments were along the London Road and on the higher reaches of Lansdown Hill including Camden and Lansdown Crescents with their subsidiary streets.

Jane Austen was born and spent a major part of her life in the Rectory at Steventon, Hampshire. This portrait is by her sister Cassandra.

Steventon Parsonage by Ben Lefroy 1820.

The Bathwick meadows had been built on, creating Laura Place and the magnificent Great Pulteney Street. However, the concentrated thirty years of building mania had ended dramatically in 1793 with a spectacular financial crash, a legacy of involvement in the Napoleonic Wars.

At the time of Jane's first recorded visit to the city she was already an accomplished, yet unpublished, author, already having written the first drafts of *Pride & Prejudice* and *Sense & Sensibility*. Her third novel, *Northanger Abbey*, was written during 1798-99 and drew from the experience of this 1797 holiday.

The happy childhood of Catherine Morland, the young heroine in *Northanger Abbey*, sounds remarkably like Jane's own life at Steventon. Catherine's appearance at seventeen is described by Jane as 'pleasing, and, when in good looks, pretty.' Miss Morland loves reading Gothic novels which were very popular at the time and sometimes she made the mistake of applying fictional plots to real life situations. Her character grows throughout the story as she is exposed to new experiences in Bath, and she gradually blossoms into a real heroine.

Jane's understanding of the mores of Bath developed further with her second visit during the summer of 1799. She was in company with her brother Edward and his family when they stayed in Queen Square. During this holiday Jane reported on encounters through a number of letters to Cassandra.

James Leigh-Perrot, Jane's uncle.

Life changed dramatically for Jane in 1801 when her father announced his decision to retire and move permanently to Bath. She is reported to have been much distressed at the news. There has been much speculation about the motives behind the Austens' decision but it did provide the two young, unmarried women with a much wider social circle and presented opportunities for family holidays by the sea.

Jane stayed with her mother at the Leigh-Perrots' in 1 Paragon while they sought a suitable residence in Bath. Cassandra was staying in Kent with their brother Edward and his family and Jane's letters to her included descriptions of the house-hunting trials.

Between May 1801 and July 1806 the Austens lived in a succession of houses in the city, firstly at 4 Sydney Gardens until the lease expired when they moved to 3 Green Park Buildings (now gone). The Rev'd George Austen died on 21 January 1805 in the house in Green Park Buildings. The Austen ladies had two more brief periods of lodging, first at 25 Gay Street and later at an unknown address in Trim Street before leaving Bath for good in 1806.

The Paragon where Jane spent her first recorded visit to Bath, staying at number 1 in 1797 with her uncle and aunt.

During her five years in Bath, Jane wrote only the first few chapters of a novel called *The Watsons*, which she later discarded. However, the experience of living here provided her with the background for her final completed novel *Persuasion*, which she began in August 1815. By this time *Sense & Sensibility*, *Pride & Prejudice* and *Mansfield Park* had been published and *Emma* was ready for publication.

In the fifteen years between writing *Northanger Abbey* and *Persuasion* both the author and the city had changed. Anne Elliot, the heroine of *Persuasion* is twenty-seven, and a mature woman, whereas the heroines from the other novels are young women at the threshold of life.

The hey-day of Bath's social scene which Mrs Austen knew as a young woman was past and the fashionable people were preferring sea-bathing resorts. The city had mostly settled to a place of retirement with private parties taking the place of the crush of assemblies so evocatively captured in *Northanger Abbey*.

After Jane left, the city continued to change. It is clear in *Persuasion* that she kept up with the news which is particularly reflected in her awareness of the clearing of the Bear Inn and stable to create Union Street which provided carriage access between the old and new town.

This illustrated guide explores the Georgian Bath Jane knew and provides a glimpse into the age of elegance in which she lived. It takes the reader through the city street by street pointing out the association of each significant house and building. It also follows in Jane's steps on excursions she made into the countryside and villages beyond the city boundaries.

Rowlandson's 1798 cartoon 'The Comforts of Bath' a scene so wonderfully captured in Northanger Abbey.

Abbey Churchyard [map D5]

In Jane Austen's time the Abbey Churchyard was called the Pump Yard and it looked a little different from the prospect that we see today. For a start there were lean-to shops around the Abbey walls and the flying buttresses and pinnacles on the Abbey are Victorian additions. Jane doesn't mention the Abbey but we must believe she attended some services here during the years she spent in the city.

On the southern side of the Abbey Churchyard is the large complex which houses the Roman Baths and the Pump Room. The Roman Baths were not a feature of Jane's world. They were discovered a century after she was here. During her time, the site was covered with houses. The demolition of several of these houses in the late nineteenth century revealed the Roman Baths which had been concealed for more than a millennium.

The present-day Pump Room is the one that Jane knew as the hub of Georgian life in the city. This is where the Subscription Book was kept. New arrivals in town would enter their names which were then published in the local newspapers. Catherine Morland found this useful in *Northanger Abbey* when she was trying to ascertain whether Henry Tilney was still in town.

Once new arrivals had added their names to the book, the Master of Ceremonies would then pay them a ceremonial visit, to inform them of the ways of Bath, in case of unfamiliarity.

Entering one's name in the Subscription Book entitled a visitor to subscribe to the assemblies and concerts in the Pump Room and Assembly Rooms and to circulating libraries. In May 1799, Jane's brother Edward entered his and his wife's name. He does not appear to have entered the names of his mother and sister as they were not published.

In the eighteenth-century the Pump Room was the social meeting point, the place to see and to be seen, to promenade, to exchange the latest information and of course to drink the health-giving water.

Part of Jane's daily routine was to accompany her uncle James Leigh-Perrot when he went to take the water. Both her uncle, and her fictional character Mr Allen, had 'a gouty constitution'. Jane draws on this experience in *Northanger Abbey* when she describes the scene: 'Mr. Allen, after drinking his glass of water, joined some gentlemen to talk over the politics of the day and compare the accounts of their newspapers; and the ladies walked about together, noticing every new face, and almost every new bonnet in the room.'

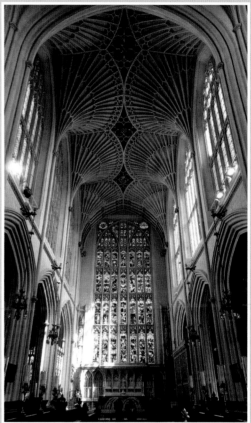

Bath Abbey's magnificent fan vaulted ceiling which Jane must have seen.

Bath Abbey dominates the eastern end of the Pump Yard. In Jane's time there were lean-to shops around the Abbey walls.

The Roman Baths which were discovered a century after Jane was here.

Jane frequently uses the Pump Room as the social meeting point to bring the characters in *Northanger Abbey* together: 'The following conversation, which took place between the two friends (Catherine Morland and Isabella Thorpe) in the Pump Room one morning, after an acquaintance of eight or nine days, is given as a specimen of their very warm attachment, and of the delicacy, discretion, originality of thought, and literary taste which marked the reasonableness of that attachment.'

The morning after meeting Henry Tilney, Catherine hurries to the Pump Room in the hopes of seeing him again but to no avail. Then Mrs Allen sees Mrs Thorpe and recognizes her as an old school friend. They are engaged in conversation when Mrs Thorpe cries: ' "Here come my dear girls." Pointing at three smart-looking females who, arm in arm, were then moving towards her. "My dear Mrs Allen, I long to introduce them; they will be so

Below left: The entrance to the Pump Room where the Subscription Book was kept for new arrivals in town to enter their names.

Below right: You can still sample the water which was described by Dickens as having a 'very strong flavour o warm flat irons'.

Right: *In addition to sampling the water you can also take your afternoon tea while listening to the Pump Room string quartet.*

Below: *The colonnade at the west end of the Pump Yard leads through to Stall Street. The modern building beyond stands on the site of the former White Hart Inn featured significantly in* Persuasion.

delighted to see you: the tallest is Isabella, my eldest; is not she a fine young woman? The others are very much admired too, but I believe Isabella is the handsomest." '

You can still sample the water but you might like to consider the description Charles Dickens gave in *Pickwick Papers* when he said you can expect a 'very strong flavour o warm flat irons'. Nowadays you can get your spa water flavoured with various fruit juices. In addition to sampling the water you can also take your afternoon tea while listening to the Pump Room string quartet.

Alfred Street [map C3]

Alfred Street runs along the southern boundary of the Upper Assembly Rooms. In a letter to Cassandra dated 5 May 1805 Jane mentions that: 'Mary Cooke did walk with us on Tuesday, and we drank tea in Alfred Street.'

Alfred House, at the end of the street, has the original Georgian ironwork complete with lantern overthrow and link snuffer. A link was a flaming torch. In Jane's time pedestrians making their way home on a moonless night could hire a 'link-boy' to lead the way. The link-boy's fee was commonly one farthing, and the torch was often made from burning pitch and tow. Tow is made of fine strands of hemp that look like brown sheep's wool after it has been combed ready for spinning. The tow was soaked in tallow (mutton fat).

Link-boys with their torches also led the way for the sedan chairs. Where possible, the link-boys would escort the fares to the chairmen. The passengers would then be carried to the door of their lodgings.

Far right: *The entrance to Alfred Street from Lansdown Road.*

Right: *Alfred House, at the end of the street, has the original Georgian ironwork complete with lantern overthrow and link snuffer.*

Bath Street [map D5]

This elegant little street Jane knew very well was completed by city architect Thomas Baldwin only six years before her visit of 1797. It was colonnaded to afford shelter to pedestrians and sedan chairmen transferring from King's and Queen's Baths down to Cross Bath. There is a wide semi-circular quadrant in front of King's Bath and in front of Cross Bath at the far end which enabled carriages to turn easily.

Cross Bath, completed by Baldwin in 1784, is today part of the new Thermae Bath Spa complex and contains a delightful little pool for up to a dozen bathers. In the photograph, Westgate Buildings are seen rising behind the Cross Bath. These buildings housed the impecunious Mrs. Smith in *Persuasion*.

Number 7, on the left, at the far end of Bath Street is today the reception/ticket office for the new Thermae Bath Spa. In the spring of 1805 Richard Buller and his wife were lodging here when Jane Austen called. Richard had been one of Rev'd George Austen's pupils at Steventon, and therefore would have been one of the boys at the rectory when Jane was growing up.

This elegant little street Jane knew very well was completed only six years before her visit of 1797.

Bath Street was colonnaded to afford shelter to pedestrians transferring between baths.

Inside Queen's Bath 1804.

Richard and Jane were of a similar age; he was born in 1776, a few months after her. In a letter dated April 1805, Jane tells her sister: 'Mr Buller had called while we were out. He left his address and I am just returned from seeing him and his wife in their lodgings at 7 Bath Street… I am afraid it must be too late for these waters to do him any good'.

Her predictions unfortunately proved to be right, Richard died the following year. He was the son of the Rt Rev'd William Buller, Bishop of Exeter and his wife Anne. Richard seems to have been a special pupil of Rev'd Austen's. When Charles Austen, Jane's younger brother left home in 1791 to join the Navy, her father reduced the number of his pupils to just Richard Buller, William Goodenough, and two others. Bishop Buller paid more than double fees for his son, which suggests he was in need of special care and attention.

*   *   *

Through her correspondence and novels we see that Jane had a lively interest in dress. Her letters are full of allusions to fashions, and ingenious ways for bringing older ones up

The Cross Bath end of Bath Street as Jane would have known it.

to date. She had little opportunity to see new fashions when she lived at Steventon so took full advantage of the retail possibilities provided by the city.

During her visit to Bath in 1799 she wrote a letter to Cassandra in which she mentions shopping in Bath Street. 'I saw some gauzes in a shop in Bath Street yesterday at only 4d. a yard, but they were not so good or so pretty as mine.' This was probably the shop which later was to feature dramatically in the annals of the Austen family. It stands on the corner of Bath Street and Stall Street and is now a shoe shop.

Soon after Jane's spring visit of 1799, an incident occured here which would cast a pall over the Leigh-Perrots' stay in the city. During August of that year, Mrs Leigh-Perrot had called in to a buy a length of black lace. With the purchase completed and the parcel wrapped Jane's aunt and uncle went on their way.

At that time the shop was owned by a Mrs Smith and run by her sister, Miss Gregory, who later that day accosted the Leigh-Perrots in the street and asked to inspect Mrs Leigh-

Today Cross Bath at the western end of Bath Street is part of the new Thermae Bath Spa complex and contains a delightful little pool for up to a dozen bathers.

Perrot's package. When she did so it was discovered that a card of white lace, worth twenty shillings, was also included in the parcel. Mrs Leigh-Perrot said the shop clerk must have accidently wrapped the white lace along with the black but Miss Gregory insisted she was guilty of shoplifting.

Mrs Leigh-Perrot forcefully denied the claim and continued home to the Paragon. After a day or two she started to receive menacing anonymous letters warning her that soon all her friends and acquaintances would be advised of the theft. Jane's aunt ignored the threats but six days later Miss Gregory and Filby the shop man went to the magistrates and swore out a warrant. A few days later Mrs Leigh-Perrot was arrested on a charge of grand larceny.

Mrs Leigh-Perrot was remanded in the county jail at Ilchester for eight months, pending trial at the March Assizes held in Taunton. Due to her station as a gentle-

woman, she was not incarcerated in the public prison, but was instead lodged with the jailer and his family which was still a grim experience.

Her devoted husband stayed by her side, regardless of the 'Vulgarity, Dirt, Noise from morning till night'. Mrs Leigh-Perrot reported on her husband's situation: 'Cleanliness has ever been his greatest delight, and yet he sees the greasy toast laid by the dirty children on his knees, and feels the small Beer trickle down his Sleeves on its way across the table unmoved.'

The seriousness of the situation should not be underestimated. At that time, theft of any item worth five shillings or more was punishable by hanging but the sentence was usually reduced to deportation to Australia for fourteen years. The trial took place on 29 March, 1800. The jury took less than fifteen minutes to return a 'not guilty' verdict.

Above left: In the spring of 1805 Jane called here at 7 Bath Street to visit her friend Richard Buller and his wife. Today it is the reception/ticket office for the Thermae Bath Spa.

Above right: The shop on the corner of Stall Street and Bath Street where Mrs Leigh-Perrot was accused of stealing a card of white lace, worth twenty shillings.

Bennett Street - Assembly Rooms [map C2]

In the middle of the eighteenth century the Assembly Rooms were at the heart of Bath's social life. Here balls and concerts were arranged with the addition of card playing for the non-dancing men.

Bath's famous 'Upper' Assembly Rooms in Bennett Street, which Jane came to know well, were opened in 1771, only a few years before her birth. They were designed by John Wood the Younger to provide for the residents of the newly built upper parts of the town who did not want to go down to the old town's Assembly Rooms.

The Upper Rooms were more modern and spacious, and reflected eighteenth-century elegance. Jane also knew the much older 'Lower Rooms' which stood near the fountain at

In the middle of the eighteenth century the Assembly Rooms were a meeting place for balls, concerts, card playing and taking tea.

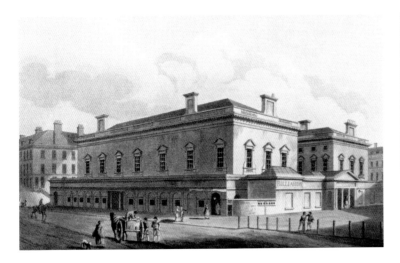

Above left: *The Upper Rooms in 1806.*

Above right: *This painting of The Cloakroom of Clifton Assembly confirms that a ballroom in full season, 'was one of the most pleasing sights that the imagination of man can conceive'.*

the end of North Parade Passage overlooking Parade Gardens. The Lower Rooms burned to the ground in 1820 and were not rebuilt.

There are three main rooms: the Ballroom and Tea Room are linked by the Octagon Room originally intended as a circulating space which could also be used for music. A new Card Room was added in 1777. In Bath's heyday dancing was very popular and balls were held at least twice a week, attracting 800 to 1,200 guests at a time, but by the turn of the century things were in decline. The fashionable set were gravitating to Brighton and other sea-bathing resorts following the lead of the Prince of Wales, and Bath was becoming a place of retirement.

In a letter dated 12 May 1801 Jane describes attending a ball in the Upper Rooms: 'In the evening, I hope you honoured my toilette and ball with a thought; I dressed myself as well as I could, and had all my finery much admired at home. By nine o'clock my uncle, aunt, and I entered the rooms, and linked Miss Winstone on to us. Before tea it was rather a dull affair; but then the before tea did not last long, for there was only one dance, danced by four couple. Think of four couple, surrounded by about an hundred people, dancing in the Upper Rooms at Bath.'

This is the only description of a Bath Assembly that survives in Jane's letters. However she makes frequent use of the rooms as a device for dramatic incident in both of the Bath novels when gathering her characters together.

The centrally situated Octagon Room was the meeting and circulating space which could also be used for music.

During evening entertainments there was an interval for tea, the cost being included in the price of a ball ticket.

In *Northanger Abbey* we have some idea of the crush of people during the height of the season: 'Mrs Allen was so long in dressing that they did not enter the ballroom till late. The season was full, the room crowded, and the two ladies squeezed in as well as they could. As for Mr Allen, he repaired directly to the card–room, and left them to enjoy a mob by themselves.'

'With more care for the safety of her new gown than for the comfort of her protégée, Mrs. Allen made her way through the throng of men by the door, as swiftly as the necessary caution would allow; Catherine, however, kept close at her side, and linked her arm too firmly within her friend's to be torn asunder by any common effort of a struggling assembly. But to her utter amazement she found that to proceed along the room was by no means the way to disengage themselves from the crowd; it seemed rather to increase as they went on, whereas she had imagined that when once fairly within the door, they should easily find seats and be able to watch the dances with perfect convenience.'

'But this was far from being the case, and though by unwearied diligence they gained even the top of the room, their situation was just the same; they saw nothing of the dancers but the high feathers of some of the ladies. Still they moved on – something better was yet in view; and by a continued exertion of strength and ingenuity they found themselves at last in the passage behind the highest bench… It was a splendid sight, and she began, for the first time that evening, to feel herself at a ball: she longed to dance, but she had not an acquaintance in the room… They were not long able, however, to enjoy the repose of the eminence they had so laboriously gained. Everybody was shortly in motion for tea, and they must squeeze out like the rest.'

A poignant scene in *Persuasion* takes place in the rooms when the Elliots attend a concert 'for the benefit of a person patronised by Lady Dalrymple' and Anne has a chance to speak to Captain Wentworth:

'Sir Walter, his two daughters, and Mrs Clay, were the earliest of all their party at the rooms in the evening; and as Lady Dalrymple must be waited for, they took their station by one of the fires in the Octagon Room. But hardly were they so settled, when the door opened again, and Captain Wentworth walked in alone. Anne was the nearest to him, and making yet a little advance, she instantly spoke. He was preparing only to bow and pass on, but her gentle "How do you do?" brought him out of the straight line to stand near her, and make enquiries in return, in spite of the formidable father and sister in the back ground.'

Modern visitors are sometimes disappointed the rooms are austere and the windows very high and very small. There were two reasons for this. Creating a space where nobody could see in and nobody could see out effectively created a sort of fantasy world where different values prevailed. The main season for balls was in the winter months and dances were held at night so there was no need for outside light. The high ceiling provided good ventilation and the light from hundreds of candles shimmering through the prisms of the chandeliers created a magical scene.

Here is how one visitor described it: 'On a ball night, in full season, when all the benches are filled with ladies in full dress, the Rooms magnificently lighted by wax, the splendour of the lustres, girandoles and the superlative charms of so many lovely women, whose natural beauties being awakened by the variety of amusements which, on all sides, surround them – renders it one of the most pleasing sights that the imagination of man can conceive.'

Today the basement of the Assembly Rooms is home to the Fashion Museum, with displays of dresses from the sixteenth century up to the present day with changing exhibitions. The rooms can be booked for balls and weddings.

Magical scene in the Assembly Rooms from the 1995 BBC film adaptation of Persuasion *starring Ciarán Hinds as Captain Frederick Wentworth and Amanda Root as Anne Elliot.*

The single-storey extension along the side of the building was a shelter for the sedan chairmen.

Brock Street remains an elegant thoroughfare linking the Circus with the Royal Crescent.

Here and there shop fronts and porches have been added to houses Jane would have known.

Brock Street [map B3]

Brock Street which links the Circus with the Royal Crescent was built by John Wood the Younger in 1767-8 in modest style to make the Royal Crescent and the Circus appear grander in contrast.

Jane mentions Brock Street in *Northanger Abbey* when Catherine Morland and the Thorpes take their Sunday walk along the Royal Crescent. John Thorpe caught up with the Tilneys, to excuse Catherine from walking with them: 'Thorpe told her it would be in vain to go after the Tilneys; they were turning the corner into Brock Street, when he had overtaken them, and were at home by this time.'

Camden Place (now Camden Crescent) [map D1]

In Jane Austen's time Camden Crescent was known as Camden Place. It is a turning off the steep incline of Landsdown Road and in the early nineteenth-century was nearly the northernmost point of the city and the highest point of its elevation.

The first stone was laid on 9 April 1787 and weighed two tons. A thought might be given to the horses that were involved when the crescent was under construction. Ironically for the haulage team the stone was inscribed 'nil desperandum'.

The crescent was built by John Eveleigh for Charles Pratt, Earl of Camden, whose crest, an elephant's head, in slightly varying format, can be seen over each of its doorways. It was a masterstroke of Jane Austen to place the impossibly superior Sir Walter Elliot in lodgings in 'a very good house in Camden Place, a lofty dignified situation, such as

'Sir Walter had taken a very good house in Camden Place, a lofty dignified situation, such as becomes a man of consequence.'

The view of Bath from the 'lofty dignified situation' of Camden Crescent.

Far left: The elephant's head crest of the Earl of Camden can be seen over each of the doorways in the crescent.

Left: *Bathwick Ferry with Camden Crescent in the background 1805. Note how the houses missing on the east end of the crescent destroys the symmetry of the crescent.*

Below: *Here the construction of the vaulted foundation plinth can be seen extending forward under the road. This levelling technique was used on a number of the developments including Green Park Buildings and the whole of Great Pulteney Street.*

becomes a man of consequence; and both he and Elizabeth were settled there, much to their satisfaction.'

From here Sir Walter could look down on everyone both metaphorically and physically. Moreover the foundations of Camden Place, in common with Sir Walter's own financial situation, were on shaky ground. As a result of a landslip only eighteen houses of the crescent, together with the whole of the left wing, were completed, leaving the central pediment disconcertingly off centre.

Jane tells us in *Persuasion* that the Elliot's house 'was undoubtedly the best in Camden Place', which suggests she had the central one with the pediment in mind: 'Their house was undoubtedly the best in Camden Place, their drawing-rooms had many decided advantages over all the others which they had either seen or heard of, and the superiority was not less in the style of the fitting-up, or the taste of the furniture. Their acquaintance was exceedingly sought after. Everybody was wanting to visit them. They had drawn back from many introductions, and still were perpetually having cards left by people of whom they knew nothing.'

Anne found it a 'toilsome' walk from the old town up Lansdown Road to Camden Place so she was pleased on the day she met an escort in the form of Admiral Croft: 'Anne was too much engaged with Lady Russell to be often walking herself; but it so happened that one morning, about a week or ten days after the Croft's arrival, it suited her best to leave her friend, or her friend's carriage, in the lower part of the town, and return alone to Camden Place, and in walking up Milsom Street she had the good fortune to meet with the Admiral.'

The Chapel Row corner house.

Opposite, clockwise
from top left:

*The exit from the Abbey
Churchyard into Cheap
Street through which the
two young men disappeared.*

*The view from Cheap Street
into Abbey Churchyard.*

*Cheap Street, far less
'impertinent' than it was in
Jane Austen's day.*

*Looking down the narrow
Union Passage towards the
Abbey.*

Chapel Row [map C4]

Princes Street runs north to the south west corner of Queen Square. On the right of this junction is 13 Queen Square and on the left corner, a few yards across the road, is the first house in Chapel Row. The Austens lodged at 13 Queen Square for a period of six weeks from 17 May to 27 June 1799 and Mrs Austen retained a great affection for 'the Square' all her life.

When the family came to look for a permanent residence in Bath eighteen months later, Jane reported: 'My mother hankers after the Square dreadfully.' Being disappointed in this plan, Mrs Austen started to consider the corner house in Chapel Row as her number one choice. It might not have such a prestigious address but it enjoys a clear view across the Square. On 3 January 1801 Jane reported to Cassandra details of her Mother's inclination:

'...above all others her wishes are at present fixed on the corner house in Chapel Row, which opens into Prince's Street. Her knowledge of it, however, is confined only to the outside, and therefore she is equally uncertain of its being really desirable as of its being to be had. In the meantime she assures you that she will do everything in her power to avoid Trim Street, although you have not expressed the fearful presentment of it which was rather expected.'

Cheap Street [map D5]

Cheap Street runs along the northern side of Abbey Churchyard. In a scene from *Northanger Abbey*, Catherine Morland is enjoying a conversation in the Pump Room with her newly found friend, the worldly Isabella Thorpe. As the young ladies are preparing to leave Isabella becomes aware of 'two odious young men' who have been staring at them for half an hour. The young men leave first and, all the while feigning lack of interest, Isabella encourages her bemused friend to chase after them as fast as they could walk.

'Half a minute conducted them through the pump-yard to the archway, opposite Union Passage; but here they were stopped. Everybody acquainted with Bath may remember the difficulties of crossing Cheap Street at this point; it is indeed a street of so impertinent a nature, so unfortunately connected with the great London and Oxford roads, and the principal inn of the city, that a day never passes in which parties of ladies, however important their business, whether in quest of pastry, millinery, or even (as in the present case) of young men, are not detained on one side or other by carriages, horsemen, or carts.'

Cheap Street is less' impertinent' than it was in Jane Austen's day, partly because the Bear, 'the principal inn' she mentions, was demolished in 1806 to create Union Street. The young men disappear along Union Passage opposite the colonnade on the north side of Abbey Churchyard.

The Circus [map C3]

The foundation stone of what was originally called the 'King's Circus', was laid on 7 February 1754. Less than four months later, with work hardly started, architect John Wood the Elder died. Wood had based his design of the Circus on Stonehenge which he had surveyed and written about at great length in his book *An Essay on Bath*.

Wood was absorbed by the idea of Druids and sought to build a Druid Temple for the eighteenth-century. The frieze, all the way round the Circus, is comprised of Masonic and Druid symbols carved into the stone. The acorns around the parapet are a reference to the

The acorns around the parapet are a reference to the legend of Prince Bladud and the fact that Druids hold the oak tree to be sacred.

The King's Circus as it appeared originally as an open paved arena.

42

Today the five massive plane trees, planted around 190 years ago, dominate the centre of the Circus.

The trees detract from the architecture but contribute to the air quality.

Druids who consider the oak tree sacred. They also allude to the legend of Prince Bladud (father of King Lear) whose pigs, when rooting for acorns, discovered the healing springs on which Bath is founded. Wallowing in the mud they were cured of the leprosy they had contracted from the princely swineherd. A statue of Bladud and his pigs can be seen in Parade Gardens.

John Wood's son, John Wood the Younger, took over after his father died but it would be a dozen years before the project was completed. There was never an intention to have a central island of grass and trees. Initially the whole arena was paved with granite sets.

One of the residents of the Circus at the turn of the nineteenth-century was a Dr Mapleton. He was known to the Austens, and lived with his wife and three daughters Jane, Marianne and Christiana at number 11. Jane Austen, who generally did not appear to have much respect for the ability of doctors, seems to have had a better opinion of him. On 19 June 1801 she wrote:

'Mrs Williams need not pride herself upon her knowledge of Dr Mapleton's success here; she knows no more than everybody else knows in Bath. There is not a physician in the place who writes so many prescriptions as he does. I cannot help wishing that Edward had not been tied down to Dr Fellowes, for, had he come disengaged, we should all have recommended Dr Mapleton; my uncle and aunt as earnestly as ourselves.'

Jane Austen made social calls here at 11 the Circus, which was home to Dr and Mrs Mapleton and their three daughters Jane, Marianne and Christiana. Note the frieze of Masonic and Druid symbols carved into the stone lintels.

The Mapletons were one of the families the Austens visited socially – and selectively according to Jane: 'I do not see the Miss Mapletons very often, but just as often as I like; we are always very glad to meet, and I do not wish to wear out our satisfaction.'

Although Jane had regard for Dr Mapleton's competence he was not able to save his own daughter Marianne. On 12 May 1802 Jane told Cassandra: 'I have bestowed three calls of inquiry on the Mapletons, and I fancy very beneficial ones to Marianne, as I am always told that she is better. I have not seen any of them. Her complaint is a bilious fever.'

Nine days later, on 21 May, the news was tragic: 'You will be sorry to hear that Marianne Mapleton's disorder has ended fatally. She was believed out of danger on Sunday, but a sudden relapse carried her off the next day. So affectionate a family must suffer severely; and many a girl on early death has been praised into an angel, I believe, on slighter pretensions to beauty, sense, and merit than Marianne.'

The Crofts had placed themselves in lodgings in Gay Street 'perfectly to Sir Walter's satisfaction'.

G

After Mr Austen's death in January 1805 at Green Park Buildings the Austen ladies moved here to 25 Gay Street.

Gay Street [map C3]

Gay Street links Queen Square to The Circus. It was designed by John Wood, the Elder in 1735 and completed by his son John Wood the Younger. About three months after her husband's death in January 1805, Mrs Austen gave up the lease on the house in Green Park Buildings and moved with her daughters to 25 Gay Street.

In *Persuasion*, Sir Walter's thoughts upon choosing Admiral Croft as the tenant of Kellynch Hall were, 'the admiral's situation in life… it was just high enough, and not too high'. He has a similar concern about the location of the Bath lodgings where Admiral and Mrs Croft might settle. He is anxious that they 'be situated in such a part of Bath as it might suit Miss Elliot and himself to visit in'. Luckily the Crofts find accommodation 'perfectly to Sir Walter's satisfaction' in Gay Street.

Gay Street is sufficiently further 'down' in the city, but not so far down that it would be a source of embarrassment for Sir Walter and Elizabeth to visit and not so 'high' as to make the address too close for comfort. Asked if they should present the Crofts to their august relations the Dalrymples in Laura Place, Elizabeth Elliot answers, 'Oh! no, I think not. . . . We had better leave the Crofts to find their own level.'

The Jane Austen Centre at 40 Gay Street is a permanent exhibition which tells the story of Jane Austen's experience of Bath and the influence that visiting and living in the city had on her and her writing.

George Street, Edgar Buildings [map C3]

Edgar Buildings stands on a raised pavement on the north side of George Street, with the pediment of its palatial façade facing directly down Milsom Street. Built around 1761, this was one of Bath's set pieces in Jane Austen's time and would be still recognisable to her. The grandiose porch below the central pediment is a Victorian addition to the entrance of the Bath Constitutional Club.

In *Northanger Abbey*, Jane places Mrs Thorpe (a long term friend of Mrs Allen) in lodgings here with her daughters Isabella, Anne and Maria. Just below, in Milsom Street, she has General Tilney in lodgings with his son and daughter Henry and Eleanor. Naturally, with the majority of characters gathered here, this location features frequently throughout the Bath section of the story.

The view south from Edgar Buildings down Milsom Street with the wooded slopes of Beechen Cliff in the distance.

Edgar Buildings stands on a raised pavement across the top of Milsom Street.

For example we learn in chapter seven that: 'a pre-engagement in Edgar's Buildings prevented James Morland accepting the invitation of one friend, and obliged him to hurry away as soon as he had satisfied the demands of the other. The time of the two parties uniting in the Octagon Room being correctly adjusted, Catherine was then left to the luxury of a raised, restless, and frightened imagination over the pages of Udolpho, lost from all worldly concerns of dressing and dinner, incapable of soothing Mrs Allen's fears on the delay of an expected dressmaker, and having only one minute in sixty to bestow even on the reflection of her own felicity, in being already engaged for the evening.'

Mrs Allen, who lives for shopping, is very pleased with her situation in Edgar Buildings as she tells Henry Tilney: 'Bath is a charming place, sir; there are so many good shops here… one can step out of doors and get a thing in five minutes.'

Looking up Milsom Street to Edgar Buildings at the top.

Scene from the 2007 film adaptation of Northanger Abbey *starring Felicity Jones as* Catherine Morland.

The shops are also a convenience for Catherine Morland: 'Towards the end of the morning, however, Catherine, having occasion for some indispensable yard of ribbon which must be bought without a moment's delay, walked out into the town, and in Bond Street overtook the second Miss Thorpe as she was loitering towards Edgar's Buildings between two of the sweetest girls in the world, who had been her dear friends all the morning. From her, she soon learned that the party to Clifton had taken place.' The following morning Catherine Morland, who had chosen instead to walk to Beechen Cliff, was eager to hear all about the excursion.

'Early the next day, a note from Isabella, speaking peace and tenderness in every line, and entreating the immediate presence of her friend on a matter of the utmost importance, hastened Catherine, in the happiest state of confidence and curiosity, to Edgar's Buildings.'

'The two youngest Miss Thorpes were by themselves in the parlour; and, on Anne's quitting it to call her sister, Catherine took the opportunity of asking the other for some particulars of their yesterday's party. Maria desired no greater pleasure than to speak of it; and Catherine immediately learnt that it had been altogether the most delightful scheme in the world, that nobody could imagine how charming it had been, and that it had been more delightful than anybody could conceive.'

Gravel Walk and Georgian Garden [map B3]

The Gravel Walk runs from Queen's Parade Place behind houses in Gay Street, The Circus and Brock Street. This secluded way was actually the route for the sedan chairmen to and from the city centre up to the Royal Crescent and Marlborough Buildings. The last remaining shelter for the chairmen still stands in Queen's Parade Place.

Jane uses Gravel Walk as the setting for the touching love scene in *Persuasion* where Anne Elliot and Captain Frederick Wentworth walk together after their renewed engagement. They need somewhere private to walk and talk and pour out their feelings. They set off through the streets of Bath to Gravel Walk and take time to stroll along this quiet way.

'... and soon words enough had passed between them to decide their direction towards the comparatively quiet and retired gravel walk, where the power of conversation would make the present hour a blessing indeed, and prepare for it all the immortality which the happiest recollections of their own future lives could bestow.'

Part way along Gravel Walk, tucked discreetly behind 4 the Circus, is a Georgian Garden, recreated to the original plan of circa 1760/1770. The garden is open to the public with free entry from 9 am to 4.30 pm.

Obliquely opposite Gravel Walk steps is the last remaining shelter for the sedan chairmen.

Steps from Queens Parade Place lead up to the Gravel Walk.

Gravel Walk runs from Queen's Parade Place behind houses in Gay Street, the Circus and Brock Street.

Part way along Gravel Walk, behind 4 the Circus, is a Georgian Garden.

Recreated to the original plan of circa 1760/1770, the garden is open to the public from 9 am to 4.30 pm and the entry is free.

Great Pulteney Street [map F4]

Great Pulteney Street is a grand thoroughfare that connects Bathwick, with the City of Bath. Commissioned by Sir William Pulteney, it was designed by the architect Thomas Baldwin and completed in 1789. The council wished to expand the city, and Sir William's estate was conveniently situated on the opposite side of the River Avon.

The access to Great Pulteney Street from the city is across Pulteney Bridge, along the short section of Argyle Street and around Laura Place, from where it stretches 1,000 feet (300 m) in a straight line down to the Holburne Museum in Sydney place. This is the grandest and widest street in Bath, at 100 feet (30 m) wide it was possible to turn a horse-drawn carriage in a single sweep.

Some of the properties were built as hotels and in *Northanger Abbey* Jane has her heroine Catherine Morland lodge in one of these with her chaperones Mr and Mrs Allen:

Great Pulteney Street stretches 1,000 feet (300 m) down a straight line to the Holburne Museum in Sydney Place.

Jane's heroine Catherine *Morland lodges in one of the hotels with her chaperones* Mr and Mrs Allen.

'They arrived at Bath. Catherine was all eager delight – her eyes were here, there, everywhere, as they approached its fine and striking environs, and afterwards drove through those streets which conducted them to the hotel. She was come to be happy, and she felt happy already… They were soon settled in comfortable lodgings in Pulteney Street.'

With the Thorpes and the Tilneys settled in the heart of the city at Edgar Buildings and Gay Street respectively, and Catherine Morland and the Allens, somewhat removed on the Bathwick Estate, there is much coming and going of people along Great Pulteney Street, on foot and in vehicles: 'Catherine, delighted by all that had passed, proceeded gaily to Pulteney Street, walking, as she concluded, with great elasticity, though she had never thought of it before.'

Later in the novel Catherine Morland is driven along the street by the scheming John Thorpe heading for the city centre: 'They passed briskly down Pulteney Street, and through Laura Place, without the exchange of many words. Thorpe talked to his horse, and she meditated, by turns, on broken promises and broken arches, phaetons and false hangings, Tilneys and trap–doors. As they entered Argyle Buildings, however, she was roused by this address from her companion, "Who is that girl who looked at you so hard as she went by?"'

Great Pulteney Street also features in *Persuasion*. Lady Russell who 'persuaded' Anne Elliot to part with Captain Wentworth some years before is no pedestrian, she goes everywhere in her carriage and, at this stage in her life, Anne never walks out for pleasure. One morning the two ladies are in Lady Russell's carriage, travelling along Great Pulteney Street, when Anne spots Captain Wentworth walking along the street. She wonders what her friend will say but Lady Russell pretends not to see him:

'The following morning Anne was out with her friend, and for the first hour, in an incessant and fearful sort of watch for him in vain; but at last, in returning down Pulteney Street, she distinguished him on the right hand pavement at such a distance as to have him in view the greater part of the street.'

'There were many other men about him, many groups walking the same way, but there was no mistaking him. She looked instinctively at Lady Russell; but not from any mad idea of her recognising him so soon as she did herself. No, it was not to be supposed that Lady Russell would perceive him till they were nearly opposite'.

'She looked at her however, from time to time, anxiously; and when the moment approached which must point him out, though not daring to look again (for her own countenance she knew was unfit to be seen), she was yet perfectly conscious of Lady Russell's eyes being turned exactly in the direction for him – of her being, in short, intently observing him.'

'At last, Lady Russell drew back her head. Now, how would she speak of him? "You will wonder," said she, "what has been fixing my eye so long; but I was looking after some window-curtains, which Lady Alicia and Mrs Frankland were telling me of last night. They described the drawing-room window-curtains of one of the houses on this side of the way, and this part of the street, as being the handsomest and best hung of any in Bath, but could not recollect the exact number, and I have been trying to find out which it could be; but I confess I can see no curtains hereabouts that answer their description."'

In 1810 the Leigh-Perrots purchased 49 Great Pulteney Street.

'Anne sighed and blushed and smiled, in pity and disdain, either at her friend or herself. The part which provoked her most, was that in all this waste of foresight and caution, she should have lost the right moment for seeing whether he saw them.'

In 1810 the ageing Leigh-Perrots no longer rented 1 Paragon but instead bought their own house at 49 Great Pulteney Street which afforded a level walk into town.

Green Park Buildings [map B5]

The Bath area of Kingsmead was developed in the 1790s to accommodate an expanding population. Green Park Buildings was a curious arrangement consisting of two straight terraces in a V-shape with the tip jutting into Kingsmead Meadows, and the river below completing the third side of the triangle. It was a pleasant situation with the meadows and the river close at hand and the houses built on an elevated a platform of vaults to counteract potential flooding.

On the evening of 5 May 1801 Jane wrote: 'When my uncle went to take his second glass of water I walked with him, and in our morning's circuit we looked at two houses in Green Park Buildings, one of which pleased me very well. We walked all over it except into the garret; the dining-room is of a comfortable size, just as large as you like to fancy it; the second room about 14 ft. square. The apartment over the drawing-room pleased me particularly, because it is divided into two, the smaller one a very nice-sized dressing-room, which upon occasion might admit a bed. The aspect is south-east. The only doubt is about the dampness of the offices, of which there were symptoms'.

Opposite: *Green Park Buildings West.*

To counteract flooding the houses were raised up on a platform of vaults extending under the road which can be seen from Green Park.

The house where the Austens lived was destroyed by bombing in 1942 but the houses along Green Park Buildings West, give us a very good idea of the type of property.

Bomb-damaged house in Green Park East.

At that time they were looking at number 12. Regarding the damp, Mr Phillips the owner offered to raise the floor in the basement kitchen but Jane realised this would simply hide the problem and not solve it.

A couple of weeks later she gave a revised opinion of the area: 'Our views on G. P. Buildings seem all at an end; the observation of the damps still remaining in the offices of an house which has been only vacated a week, with reports of discontented families and putrid fevers, has given the coup de grace. We have now nothing in view. When you arrive, we will at least have the pleasure of examining some of these putrefying houses again; they are so very desirable in size and situation, that there is some satisfaction in spending ten minutes within them.'

Eventually the Austens decided they could afford to live in a more convenient part of town and took a lease on 4 Sydney Place opposite the Sydney Pleasure Gardens. They stayed here until the lease expired in 1804 when the search for a new house began. They finally, though reluctantly, settled on 3 Green Park Buildings East which was ultimately destroyed in a two-night enemy bombing raid in June 1942.

Although the house in which the Austens lived no longer exists other houses along Green Park Buildings West give a very good idea of how the property would have appeared. Number 3 Green Park Buildings East was the scene of the saddest event in Jane's life: the death of her father in January 1805, coming hard on the news of the death of her great friend, Mrs Lefroy on 16 December 1804, Jane's twenty-ninth birthday.

The two letters Jane was impelled to write to her brother Frank at this time still exist. They make for painful reading: she being so correct but also anxious for Frank having to receive by letter the news of the death of his excellent father:

'His tenderness as a Father, who can do justice to? My Mother is tolerably well; she bears up with great fortitude, but I fear her health must suffer under such a shock. An express was sent for James, and he arrived here this morning before eight o'clock.-The Funeral is to be on Saturday, at Walcot Church.'

The first house in the road which Jane would have passed each time she went into town.

'The Serenity of the Corpse is most delightful! It preserves the sweet, benevolent smile which always distinguished him. They kindly press my Mother to remove to Steventon as soon as it is all over, but I do not believe she will leave Bath at present. We must have this house for three months longer, and here we shall probably stay till the end of that time. We all unite in Love, and I am affec:'y Yours JA.'

Mrs Austen gave up the lease on the house in Green Park Buildings sometime towards the end of March and moved with Cassandra and Jane to 25 Gay Street.

Hetling Court [map D5]

Hetling Court is a quiet little corner tucked away behind the Cross Bath at the end of Bath Street. Jane's brother Edward came here in the early summer of 1799 on the instruction of his doctor. He had been feeling unwell and he was advised to visit Bath.

Edward was the third of the eight Austen children. He was born on 7 October 1767 at Deane in Hampshire. As a youth he was adopted by Thomas and Catherine Knight, wealthy relatives of his father. Edward later changed his surname to Knight and lived on the Kentish estate he had inherited at Godmersham where he brought up his own family.

Before leaving Kent, Edward's physician had referred him to Dr Fellowes, one of the most fashionable consultants in Bath. Physician Extraordinary to the Prince of Wales, Fellowes lived three doors along from the Leigh-Perrots in the Paragon. He advised Edward to drink at the Hetling Pump and to bathe occasionally in the Hot Bath to which the pump was attached.

Below left: Hetling Court is a quiet little corner tucked away behind the Cross Bath at the end of Bath Street.

Below right: The Hetling Pump Room is now used as the information centre for the new Thermae Bath Spa which can be seen in the background of the photograph.

Edward was thirty-one when he came to Bath, accompanied by his wife and two of their children, Fanny and Edward. Jane and Mrs Austen were also invited and four of Jane's chatty letters survive from this time containing a number of references to Edward's health and the various doctors he consulted.

Edward Austen came here in the early summer of 1799 to drink at the Hetling Pump and occasionally to bathe in the attached Hot Bath.

On 2 June 1799 Jane gave a progress report to Cassandra: 'What must I tell you of Edward? Truth or falsehood. I will try the former, and you may choose for yourself another time. He was better yesterday than he had been for two or three days before – about as well as while he was at Steventon. He drinks at the Hetling Pump, is to bathe to-morrow, and try electricity on Tuesday. He proposed the latter himself to Dr Fellowes, who made no objection to it, but I fancy we are all unanimous in expecting no advantage from it.'

Edward's physician, Dr Fellowes, lived here in the Paragon, three doors up from the Leigh-Perrots.

The electrical treatment involved brushing the skin with metal rods through which flowed a mild current. Known as Perkins Tractors, these were very fashionable and supposed to cure a variety of ailments. Jane was right to be sceptical because a year later another Bath doctor, John Haygarth, debunked the whole idea by using wooden tractors painted to look like metal. These proved just as effective and by doing so he discovered the placebo effect.

Just over a week later Jane updated the information: 'Edward has been pretty well for this last week, and as the waters have never *dis*agreed with him in any respect, we are inclined to hope that he will derive advantage from them in the end. Everybody encourages us in this expectation, for they all say that the effect of the waters cannot be negative, and many are the instances in which their benefit is felt afterwards more than on the spot. He is more comfortable here than I thought he would be'.

Edward could have been suffering from some kind of food poisoning. On 19 June Jane reported: 'Edward has seen the apothecary [dispensing chemist] to whom Dr Millman recommended him, a sensible, intelligent man, since I began this, and he attributes his present little feverish indisposition to his having ate something unsuited to his stomach. I do not understand that Mr Anderton suspects the gout at all; the occasional particular glow in the hands and feet, which we considered as a symptom of that disorder, he only calls the effect of the water in promoting a better circulation of the blood.'

Lansdown Crescent [map - just beyond C1]

One of the finest architectural features of Lansdown Hill is Lansdown Crescent. It is a left turn just off the top of the map. There are still fine views to be had from here and the air is sweeter. In *Persuasion*, Mr Elliot, Anne's cousin and heir to Kellynch is dining one evening in Lansdown Crescent and calls late at his uncle's house just below in Camden Crescent:

'A knock at the door! and so late! It was ten o'clock. Could it be Mr Elliot? They knew he was to dine in Lansdown Crescent. It was possible that he might stop in his way home to ask them how they did. They could think of no one else. Mrs Clay decidedly thought it Mr Elliot's knock. Mrs Clay was right. With all the state which a butler and foot-boy could give, Mr Elliot was ushered into the room.'

The Austens used to socialise with the Chamberlayne family who lived at 19 Lansdown Crescent as we learn from a letter of 5 May 1801. 'We have had Mrs Lillingstone and the Chamberlaynes to call on us. My mother was very much struck with the odd looks of the two latter; *I* have only seen *her*. Mrs Busby drinks tea and plays at cribbage here to-morrow; and on Friday, I believe, we go to the Chamberlaynes. Last night we walked by the Canal.'

Opposite: *In* Northanger Abbey, *John Thorpe tricked Catherine Morland with a promise to ride out with him up Lansdown Hill.*

The elegant Lansdown Crescent with its fine views where Mr Elliot, heir to Kellynch, dined before calling late on his cousins.

Above left: *The Austens used to socialise with the Chamberlayne family who lived here at 19 Lansdown Crescent.*

Above right: *3 Lansdown Road, home of Jane's friend Miss Irvine.*

There are also references in Jane's letters to long walks she took with Mrs Chamberlayne. On 12 May 1801 she writes: 'My uncle has quite got the better of his lameness, or at least his walking with a stick is the only remains of it. He and I are soon to take the long-planned walk to the Cassoon [sic], and on Friday we are all to accompany Mrs Chamberlayne and Miss Langley to Weston.' The 'Caisson' was a lock system on the Somerset Coal Canal which Mr Leigh-Perrot was keen to see but never quite managed it.

The Belmont Area of Landsdown Road [map 3D]

Belmont is the name given to a steep section of Lansdown Road which stands roughly parallel to the Royal Crescent. On ball nights this area would have been crowded with ascending and descending carriages turning into Bennett Street and Alfred Street on route for the Upper Assembly Rooms.

In *Persuasion*, Anne Elliot had to pass this way from her lodgings in Camden Place (now Camden Crescent) to and from the city centre. Most often she was a passenger in Lady Russell's carriage but one morning it suited her to be dropped in the lower part of town, presumably to do some shopping. On her way back she met Admiral Croft in Milsom Street and the Admiral volunteered to escort her home to Camden Place. On the walk he tells her he has something to communicate, but at first he talks of other things:

'When they were got a little farther, Anne ventured to press again for what he had to communicate. She hoped when clear of Milsom Street to have her curiosity gratified; but she was still obliged to wait, for the Admiral had made up his mind not to begin till they had gained the greater space and quiet of Belmont; and as she was not really Mrs. Croft, she must let him have his own way.'

The road is very steep here and one can imagine Admiral Croft catching his breath before he speaks: "'Well, now you shall hear something that will surprise you. But first of all, you must tell me the name of the young lady I am going to talk about. That young lady, you know, that we have all been so concerned for. The Miss Musgrove that all this has been happening to. Her Christian name: I always forget her Christian name.'"

This impressive development of twenty houses, sitting above the raised pavement in the Lansdown area of Belmont, was completed in 1773.

Laura Place was designed as an irregular diamond-shaped quadrangle to join four streets of differing widths.

Number 1 Henrietta Street features in the Austen family history and Jane's correspondence.

The fountain, which now stands at the centre was not part of the original plan but added in the nineteenth century.

Laura Place [map E4]

Laura Place is part of the Bathwick development which became known as 'Bath New Town' and is located to the east of the city on the opposite side of the River Avon. It is accessed by crossing Pulteney Bridge and traversing the short length of Argyle Street (formerly Argyle Buildings). Built by Thomas Baldwin and John Eveleigh between 1788 and 1794, Laura Place was designed as an irregular quadrangle to join four streets of differing widths.

In Jane's time Laura Place was a completely open area. The fountain, which now stands at the centre, was not part of the original plan but added in the nineteenth-century. In January 1801, during the Austens' initial house hunting phase, the possibility of securing lodgings in this vicinity was much in the family's consciousness.

Rev'd George Austen, Jane's father, rather fancied living in a house in one of the two side streets leading off from the quadrangle. However, father and daughter do not seem to have been on the same economic wavelength. On 3 January Jane wrote to her sister: 'The houses in the streets near Laura Place I should expect to be above our price' and she was right.

Eleven days later, on 14 January, she reports that her father still seems to be keen on the idea: 'At present the environs of Laura Place seem to be his choice. His views on the subject are much advanced since I came home; he grows quite ambitious, and actually requires now a comfortable and a creditable-looking house.'

The following week she wrote again to Cassandra: 'I join with you in wishing for the environs of Laura Place, but do not venture to expect it. My mother hankers after the Square dreadfully, and it is but natural to suppose that my uncle will take her part. It would be very pleasant to be near Sydney Gardens; we might go into the labyrinth every day.' By 'the Square', Jane is referring to Queen Square but ultimately the family settled on a house in Sydney Place so Jane had her wish to be near the gardens.

When Rev'd George Austen originally declared a liking for the side streets leading off Laura Place he did not specify a preference for either Henrietta or Johnstone Street, which join the spacious diamond-shaped area at the north and south points respectively. As a result of an economic slump, mainly due to war with France, neither was ever completed as originally planned.

Johnstone Street, named after the owner of the land, William Johnstone Pulteney, was intended to be much longer and lead to a great square which would have stood on what is now the recreation ground and rugby club pitch.

Henrietta Street running north from Laura Place forms the western boundary of Henrietta Park. This street was named after Henrietta Laura Pulteney, William's daughter, who laid the first stone of the development in 1788 when Jane Austen was thirteen.

Henrietta Laura Pulteney, for whom Henrietta Street is named, was the only child of wealthy William Johnstone Pulteney. She later became the 1st Countess of Bath.

Johnstone Street was intended to be much longer and lead to a great square on land now occupied by the recreation ground and rugby club.

The wooded hills in the background of the photograph are Claverton Down where John Thorpe took Catherine Morland for a ride in his newly acquired gig.

The house at 1 Henrietta Street does feature later in the Austen family history and Jane's correspondence. Her brother Edward had married Elizabeth Bridges and his mother-in-law, Lady Bridges, stayed here with her daughter Louisa and her son Henry and his family when she came to Bath for her health.

Also in the party was Lady Bridges's orphaned granddaughter, Fanny Cage. They stayed first at the White Hart Inn while lodgings were found. On 15 September 1813 Jane wrote to Cassandra from Edward's home in Kent:

'Now for Bath. Poor F. Cage has suffered a good deal from her accident. The noise of the White Hart was terrible to her. They will keep her quiet, I dare say. *She* is not so much delighted with the place as the rest of the party; probably, as she says herself, from having been less well, but she thinks she should like it better in the season. The streets are very empty now, and the shops not so gay as she expected. They are at No. 1 Henrietta Street, the corner of Laura Place, and have no acquaintance at present but the Bramstons.'

'Lady Bridges drinks at the Cross Bath, her son at the Hot, and Louisa is going to bathe. Dr Parry seems to be half starving Mr Bridges, for he is restricted to much such a diet as James's bread, water and meat, and is never to eat so much of that as he wishes, and he is to walk a great deal – walk till he drops, I believe gout or no gout. It really is to that purpose. I have not exaggerated'.

During the three-plus years the Austens lived in Sydney Gardens Jane frequently passed through Laura Place on her walks to and from the city centre. It was still in her thoughts a few years later when the family had left Bath for good and she sat down at her writing table in Chawton Cottage to begin *Persuasion*.

As the characters came to her she positioned them in Bath locations in accordance with their wealth and status details which her readers would have perfectly understood. We learn that, The Dowager Viscountess Dalrymple and her daughter, The Honourable Miss Carteret had 'taken a house, for three months, in Laura Place, and would be living in style'. This is further confirmation that Rev'd George Austen had been hankering for a house above his means.

From her name and title we are able to form conclusions about Lady Dalrymple's situation. 'Dowager' means she is a wealthy widow, holding a 'dower' which is a title or property derived from her deceased husband. 'Viscountess' means that her husband was a viscount; which is higher up the scale than the mere baronet like Sir Walter Elliot. Other characters in the novel address her simply as Lady Dalrymple. The reason she has a different surname from her daughter is because Dalrymple is the name that goes with the title. Carteret is their actual family name.

Lady Dalrymple and Miss Carteret inside the Assembly Rooms escorted by Mr Elliot and Colonel Wallis, illustrated by Charles Brock.

The Dowager Viscountess Dalrymple, despite her portentous name doesn't feature very much in the story. Her presence is merely to reveal the true nature of the other characters: Anne judges people's worth by their deeds and actions whereas the snobbery of Sir Walter and Elizabeth becomes fawning when they meet with someone who outranks them.

Lady Dalrymple had been at Bath the year before: '… and Lady Russell had heard her spoken of as a charming woman. It was very desirable that the connexion should be renewed, if it could be done, without any compromise of propriety on the side of the Elliots.'

'Sir Walter, however, would choose his own means, and at last wrote a very fine letter of ample explanation, regret, and entreaty, to his right honourable cousin. Neither Lady Russell nor Mr Elliot could admire the letter; but it did all that was wanted, in bringing three lines of scrawl from the Dowager Viscountess. "She was very much honoured, and should be happy in their acquaintance." The toils of the business were over, the sweets began. They visited in Laura Place, they had the cards of Dowager Viscountess Dalrymple, and the Honourable Miss Carteret, to be arranged wherever they might be most visible: and "Our cousins in Laura Place,"—"Our cousin, Lady Dalrymple and Miss Carteret," were talked of to everybody.'

Jane had more than one reason to position Lady Dalrymple in Laura Place. First its position just across the river and a little removed from the centre of things could be seen to be aloof and standoffish. Second, the houses in Laura Place had the unusual advantage of two water closets! The other characters meet in the house in Laura Place when Lady Dalrymple holds a benefit concert. The scene is one of much emotion for both Anne and Captain Wentworth.

When the Austens lived in Sydney Place they worshipped at Laura Chapel behind the houses in Henrietta Street just off Laura Place. This was one of the most fashionable places of worship in Bath. In 1813, the *Improved Bath Guide* described it as: 'an elegant, commodious building, and rendered comfortable in the winter season by fires in the recesses.' It was demolished in 1909 and only the arched entrances remain.

When the Austens lived in Sydney Place they worshipped at Laura Chapel which stood behind houses in Henrietta Street.

Marlborough Buildings [map A2]

Marlborough Buildings, a magnificent terrace of thirty four Georgian town houses, was developed around 1790. The houses are built on only one side of the road which rises from the Victoria Park main entrance to Weston Road. The front elevation of the terrace lies at a right angle to the Royal Crescent. To the rear are uninterrupted views to Victoria Park which was open common land in Jane's time.

The fact that the common land could not be built on contributes to Marlborough Buildings remaining a desirable address today, just as when it was sought after by members of the Georgian gentry. Throughout *Persuasion* we learn the importance of a good address when *Sir Walter Elliot* makes value judgements on Westgate Buildings, Laura Place and Gay Street.

This magnificent terrace of thirty-four Georgian town houses was developed around 1790.

From this aerial photograph can be seen the rear elevation of Marlborough Buildings lying at right-angles to the Royal Crescent.

Jane expertly uses the location of Marlborough Buildings when she places Colonel and Mrs. Wallis here. The houses are on the same 'level' as those in the Royal Crescent and the Circus but they stand slightly stage-left of the main action, as do the Wallises. They are facilitators, just as we have seen with Lady Dalrymple and her Laura Place lodgings. Both are seen to be 'living in style'. For Sir Walter the Wallises also had the distinct advantage of being good looking. Mrs Wallis was said to be 'an excessively pretty woman'.

'Colonel Wallis had been so impatient to be introduced to them! and Mr Elliot so anxious that he should! and there was a Mrs Wallis, at present known only to them by description, as she was in daily expectation of her confinement; but Mr Elliot spoke of her as "a most charming woman, quite worthy of being known in Camden Place," and as soon as she recovered they were to be acquainted.'

When Mr Elliot, wants to re-establish a relationship with Sir Walter, he uses his friend Colonel Wallis as a go-between to communicate to the baronet the extenuating circumstances of his first marriage.

'The circumstances of his marriage, too, were found to admit of much extenuation. This was an article not to be entered on by himself; but a very intimate friend of his, a Colonel Wallis, a highly respectable man, perfectly the gentleman (and not an ill-looking man, Sir Walter added), who was living in very good style in Marlborough Buildings, and had, at his own particular request, been admitted to their acquaintance through Mr Elliot, had mentioned one or two things relative to the marriage, which made a material difference in the discredit of it.'

Mr Elliot, who knows that for Sir Walter location and good looks have the upper hand over sensible judgment, seduces him with a mixture of lies and flattery to the extent that in Camden Crescent: 'Mr Elliot, and his friends in Marlborough Buildings, were talked of the whole evening.'

Below left: *The houses are built on only one side of the road which rises from the Victoria Park main entrance to Weston Road.*

Below right: *Marlborough Buildings in 1805.*

Milsom Street

In 1762, when Jane's mother was living in Bath prior to her marriage, there was great construction activity extending the city northwards from its medieval centre. The buildings in Milsom Street, that Jane would later come to appreciate as shops, were originally grand town houses.

The buildings were erected on a piece of ground known as 'Milsom's Garden', at a time, when the street was quiet and refined and far removed from the hurly-burly of the down town area. The leases on the properties stipulated they should not be used for trade but eight years later, in 1770, an advertisement placed in the *Bath Chronicle* by bookseller, Andrew Tennant, advised his customers that he had moved his business from Abbey Churchyard to 'the large shop at the corner house at the top of Milsom Street'.

The following year, Mrs Ford thanked her 'many indulging friends' who had patronised her milliner's shop in Milsom Street, which she was handing over to her niece, Mary Plura. The trend continued and by the end of the century Milsom Street had already earned its reputation as Bath's most fashionable shopping street. Even Prince Charles had a retail outlet at its centre. His 'Highgrove Shop' which sold a range of beautiful and unusual gifts traded for a number of years.

As might be expected, Jane makes good use of the Milsom Street shops and lodgings as literary locations in both *Northanger Abbey* and *Persuasion*. The importance of where one stays in Bath is hinted at by Mrs Allen in *Northanger Abbey*. Speaking to Catherine Morland of General Tilney's lodgings, she says they: 'were taken the very day after he left them, Catherine. But no wonder; Milsom Street you know.'

General Tilney was lodging in Milsom Street with his son Henry and daughter Eleanor. Catherine Morland had earlier found the address where they were staying by consulting the 'New Arrivals Book' in the Pump Room.

Charles Brock's illustration of Colonel Wallis and Sir Walter Elliot strolling in Milsom Street.

The street is also mentioned by Isabella Thorpe in her frivolous conversation with Catherine: "I have an hundred things to say to you. In the first place, I was so afraid it would rain this morning, just as I wanted to set off; it looked very showery, and that would have thrown me into agonies! Do you know, I saw the prettiest hat you can imagine, in a shop window in Milsom-street just now – very like yours, only with coquelicot ribbons instead of green; I quite longed for it. But, my dearest Catherine, what have you been doing with yourself all this morning? – Have you gone on with Udolpho?"'

Coquelicot refers to the colour red and is the French name for regular corn or field poppies. In Regency times, Paris was the fashion capital of the civilized world and French fashions the epitome of chic, so French names abounded in all matters of apparel. Coquelicot was at the height of fashion during Jane's first visit to Bath. However it was such a bold colour that for well brought up young ladies it was permissible only for trimmings or accessories.

One dramatic scene in *Persuasion* occurs in Molland's Pastry Shop in Milsom Street where the ladies seek temporary shelter: 'Mr Elliot was attending his two cousins and Mrs Clay. They were in Milsom Street. It began to rain, not much, but enough to make shelter desirable for women…'

They were discussing who should travel home with Lady Russell and it was decided that: 'Mrs Clay should be of the party in the carriage; and they had just reached this point, when Anne, as she sat near the window, descried, most decidedly and distinctly, Captain Wentworth walking down the street.'

Captain Wentworth entered the shop and was covered in confusion when he saw Anne. After a moment's pause he said: '"Though I came only yesterday, I have equipped myself

Below left: By the end of the eighteenth century Milsom Street had already earned its reputation as Bath's most fashionable shopping street.

Below right: The former Molland's Pastry Shop is now 'East', a ladies fashion shop.

properly for Bath already, you see," (pointing to a new umbrella); "I wish you would make use of it, if you are determined to walk; though I think it would be more prudent to let me get you a chair."

By his momentary embarrassment Anne realizes that Captain Wentworth is still interested in her. However, she declines his offer and walks off with Mr Elliot, leaving the captain overcome with jealousy. Molland's Pastry Shop is now a ladies fashion shop. In 1804 it had been run by the baker Nicholas Molland and taken over by his wife when he died.

The other business in Milsom Street featured in the story is the print shop whose window display held Admiral Croft's attention: 'He was standing by himself at a printshop window, with his hands behind him, in earnest contemplation of some print, and she not only might have passed him unseen, but was obliged to touch as well as address him before she could catch his notice... "I wonder where that boat was built!" (laughing heartily); "I would not venture over a horsepond in it. Well," (turning away), now, where are you bound? Can I go anywhere for you, or with you? Can I be of any use?"'

'He was standing by himself at a print shop window, with his hands behind him, in earnest contemplation of some print...'

The modern shop front at 35 Milsom Street where in Jane Austen's day print seller Joseph Fasana had his business.

There were several Milsom Street businesses selling prints in 1805 including booksellers, auctioneers and circulating libraries. However, there was a print seller, Joseph Fasana who traded from 35 Milsom Street in Jane Austen's day. The shop, which fits neatly with the description in *Persuasion* is opposite Jolly's Department Store. Above the first-floor windows can be seen the words 'Brush Manufactory' dating from the 1850s when John Strawbridge had his business here.

New King Street [map B4]

New King Street is not one of Bath's show pieces of grand terraces. The dwellings here represent the middle grade Georgian town houses, typical of the homes of artisans and tradesmen of the city in the eighteenth and nineteenth centuries. However, when the Austens were house hunting in the spring of 1801, Jane's aunt Mrs Leigh-Perrot, was keen to recommend it to her husband's poor relations.

In a letter to Cassandra written in May 1801 Jane said: 'I fancy we are to have a house in Seymour Street, or thereabouts. My uncle and aunt both like the situation. I was glad to hear the former talk of all the houses in New King Street as too small; it was my own idea of them. I had not been two minutes in the dining-room before he questioned me with all

In May 1801 Jane tells Cassandra: 'I went with my mother to help look at some houses in New King Street, towards which she felt some kind of inclination.'

19 New King Street where William Herschel lived with his sister Caroline towards the end of the 1700s.

In 1780 Sir Frederick William Herschel was appointed director of the Bath orchestra, with his sister often appearing as soprano soloist. In addition to the oboe, Herschel played the violin, harpsichord and organ. He composed numerous musical works including 24 symphonies.

his customary eager interest about Frank and Charles, their views and intentions. I did my best to give information.' Frank and Charles were two of Jane's brothers who were serving overseas as officers in the Royal Navy.

Jane's elder brother Francis (Frank) served with Nelson at the time of the Battle of Trafalgar but was annoyed he was not able to be present at the engagement because Nelson had sent him on a mission to collect stores from Morocco. Despite this disappointment, Frank went on to have a dazzling naval career eventually rising to the rank of Admiral of the Fleet and being knighted for his services.

Jane's uncle George Leigh-Perrot's 'customary eager interest about Frank and Charles' would eventually have been well satisfied because Charles, Jane's younger brother, also did well in the navy reaching the rank of Rear Admiral.

In *Persuasion* it is obvious that Jane was proud of the character and achievements of her two sailor brothers. In the very last sentence of the novel she reveals Anne Elliot's sentiments: 'She gloried in being a sailor's wife, but she must pay the tax of quick alarm for belonging to that profession which is, if possible, more distinguished in its domestic virtues than in its national importance.'

Later in her 1801 letter Jane was more specific about New King Street: 'After they left us I went with my mother to help look at some houses in New King Street, towards which she felt some kind of inclination, but their size has now satisfied her. They were smaller than I expected to find them; one in particular out of the two was quite monstrously little; the best of the sitting-rooms not so large as the little parlour at Steventon, and the second room in every floor about capacious enough to admit a very small single bed.'

Interestingly for us we are able to check out the situation of the houses for ourselves because one of them, number 19, is open to the public. It is a museum to the astronomer William Herschel and his sister Caroline. Laid out over five floors with two reception rooms on the ground and first floors. There is also a basement with kitchen, parlour and workshop.

* * *

Towards the end of the time the Herschels lived in New King Street a tragedy occurred in the house next door but one. Edmund Nelson, Lord Nelson's widowed father, suffered poor health and came to Bath to take the waters and escape the Norfolk winters. He used to lodge at 17 New King Street and in 1783 was joined there by his daughter Ann.

Ann entered the social life at Bath and danced at the Upper Rooms but fell victim to a potential hazard of these events. The dances were mostly held on winter nights and the young ladies wore thin muslin dresses. Inside the crowded ballrooms, with their massive candlelit chandeliers, it became excessively hot. Revellers returning home, even wrapped in their pelisses and capes, had to walk or travel in unheated carriages or sedan chairs.

Forty years earlier, John Wood the elder recognised there was danger throughout the year if people were exposed to draughts or extreme changes in temperature. In his proposal and plans for the Lower Assembly Rooms he said:

'… the strictest Regard has been had to place the Doors and Windows, so as to prevent People taking Cold; to contrive Apertures in the Ball-Room to let in any Quantity of Air that may be necessary in Summer; and to make the Entrance to that Room so as that people returning out of it may go through a passage into an Anti-Chamber to cool themselves before they enter the Hall to take their Chairs, or to go out into the Street to take their Coaches.'

Poor Ann Nelson caught a chill leaving the ballroom and pneumonia set in. She died on 15 November 1783 at her father's lodgings in New King Street. She was buried in the peaceful little churchyard of St Swithun, Bathford.

In later life Lord Nelson's father, Reverend Edmund Nelson, spent the winters in Bath lodging at 17 New King Street.

North Parade [map E5]

The historic terrace of North Parade, built around 1741 by John Wood the Elder was designed, as the name suggests, for promenading. During the middle of the eighteenth-century, the Bath parades were where you came for gentle exercise but more importantly, to see and be seen.

In 1742, Wood wrote that, 'when noon approaches and church is over some of the company appear on the Grand Parade and other public walks where a rotation of walking about is continued for about two hours… there are others who divert themselves with… walking in Queen Square, and in the meadows round the city.'

In Jane's time North Parade stopped short at the river, just as South Parade does today. The first bridge was not built until 1836. It was made of cast iron on stone abutments, with lodges and staircases. The bridge you see today replaced the earlier one in 1936 and is constructed completely in stone.

North Parade in 1804. The edge of the building just creeping in to the left of the picture is the original Lower Assembly Rooms. The hills in the background are Claverton Down.

The original concept behind North Parade was to include it as part of a development to be called Royal Forum which would have comprised North Parade, South Parade, Pierrepont Street and Duke Street but the idea was never realised. Many of the original houses in North Parade are now hotels and shops whilst some remain as private residences.

North Parade Buildings looking west from the bridge.

Old Bond Street [map D4]

In Jane Austen's time New Bond Street did not exist. Instead there was a yard accessed by a narrow alley called Frog Lane. The view south from Upper Borough Walls in 1805 was entirely different. Here was the stable yard of the Bear Inn, busy with horses and the activity of grooms, ostlers, carriages and coaches. This was all swept away to provide space for the present day wide thoroughfare of Union Street.

When Jane mentions Bond Street, she is referring to the shopping street we know as Old Bond Street which is the southern extension of Milsom Street, ending at a 'T' junction with Upper Borough Walls.

This is where characters in both Bath novels came to shop. In *Northanger Abbey* we see Catherine Morland hurrying to a milliner's shop: 'Catherine, having occasion for some indispensable yard of ribbon which must be bought without a moment's delay, walked out into the town, and in Bond Street overtook the second Miss Thorpe as she was loitering towards Edgar's Buildings between two of the sweetest girls in the world, who had been her dear friends all the morning.'

When Jane mentions Bond Street, she is referring to the shopping street we know as Old Bond Street, leading from Upper Borough Walls to the southern end of Milsom Street.

This area is where characters in both Bath novels come to shop.

Interior of Drury Lane Theatre, London 1808. Although on a more modest scale, the Old Orchard Theatre Bath was the first provincial theatre to be granted a Royal Patent.

In *Persuasion,* Sir Walter Elliot was engaged in people watching from inside a shop on Old Bond Street: 'Sir Walter thought much of Mrs Wallis; she was said to be an excessively pretty woman, beautiful. He longed to see her. He hoped she might make some amends for the many very plain faces he was continually passing in the streets.'

'The worst of Bath was the number of its plain women. He did not mean to say that there were no pretty women, but the number of the plain was out of all proportion. He had frequently observed, as he walked, that one handsome face would be followed by thirty, or five-and-thirty frights; and once, as he had stood in a shop on Bond Street, he had counted eighty-seven women go by, one after another, without there being a tolerable face among them.'

'It had been a frosty morning, to be sure, a sharp frost, which hardly one woman in a thousand could stand the test of. But still, there certainly were a dreadful multitude of ugly women in Bath; and as for the men! they were infinitely worse.'

Old Orchard Street [map E6]

A colonnade arch on the western side of Pierrepont Street leads through to Old Orchard Street, a quiet forgotten backwater that is still paved with pennant stone sets. The land was once the orchard of a Benedictine Abbey, hence the street name.

At the bottom of the street, the building on the left was formerly the Old Theatre Royal. John Wood the Elder who developed the site in 1750 hired Thomas Jelly, one of Bath's leading builders, to undertake the construction. The project was a great success and by 1768 the Old Orchard was the first theatre outside London to be granted a Royal Patent. For a time it was the country's most fashionable provincial theatre.

Opposite: This colonnade arch on the western side of Pierrepont Street leads through to Old Orchard Street, a quiet forgotten backwater that is still paved with pennant stone sets.

Jane's parents were courting in Bath during the 1760s so it is more than possible that Rev'd George Austen would have taken his fiancée to see a play here. Jane herself visited the theatre on 22 June 1799 and saw *The Birthday* by Charles Dibden. The practice at that time was to stage two plays per night, the second was generally a comedy for light relief, on this occasion *Bluebeard*.

During Jane's five winters' residence in the city between 1801 and 1806 she would have had altogether six separate opportunities to attend performances at the Old Orchard of *Lovers Vows*, the play so integral to the plot of *Mansfield Park*.

Jane Austen and her characters in Northanger Abbey *attended this historic theatre which is now a Masonic Lodge.*

Old Orchard was the first theatre outside London to be granted a Royal Patent.

Jane uses the experience of being in the Orchard Theatre audience in *Northanger Abbey* when Catherine Morland comes here for the evening. She makes it clear that people came to the theatre as much to be seen as to enjoy the official entertainment:

'The Allens, Thorpes, and Morlands all met in the evening at the theatre; and, as Catherine and Isabella sat together, there was then an opportunity for the latter to utter some few of the many thousand things which had been collecting within her for communication in the immeasurable length of time which had divided them.'

John Thorpe's dashing about engaging people in conversation and the chattering of Catherine Morland and Isabella Thorpe is typical of what went on: '"Oh, heavens! My beloved Catherine, have I got you at last?" was her address on Catherine's entering the box and sitting by her. "Now, Mr Morland," for he was close to her on the other side, "I shall not speak another word to you all the rest of the evening; so I charge you not to expect it."'

Catherine is vexed to find Henry Tilney was not at the play and then she described her anxiety when, at the beginning of the fifth act, she suddenly saw General Tilney and Henry joining the party in the box opposite. It is here that General Tilney first catches sight of Catherine Morland and, misled by John Thorpe's eulogies about her supposed fortune, invites her to Northanger Abbey.

'The play concluded – the curtain fell – Henry Tilney was no longer to be seen where he had hitherto sat, but his father remained, and perhaps he might be now coming round to their box. She was right; in a few minutes he appeared, and, making his way through the then thinning rows, spoke with like calm politeness to Mrs Allen and her friend.'

It is hard to believe now but Old Orchard Street was one of the busiest and most fashionable streets in the city. By 1781 a new coach road had been built to connect with the bottom of it. The street ended at the theatre and steps led down to a paved parking area with room for around fifty or sixty carriages. Beyond this were open fields and orchards stretching to the river with the wooded slopes of Beechen Cliff as a backdrop.

Sarah Siddons, seen here as the Tragic Muse by Joshua Reynolds, owned the theatre for four years with her husband and sister.

Theatre boxes were booked at the 'box office', but the way theatre-goers were sure of reserving an individual evening seat in the auditorium was to send servants along in the afternoon to sit on it. Playbills at the time recommended that: 'Ladies and gentlemen are desired to send their servants to keep places by half an hour after 4 o'clock'. The servants naturally got bored and there are reports of them behaving very badly by talking extremely loudly and shouting rude remarks to each other.

Despite major alterations and extensions in 1774, the old theatre eventually proved too small to cater for the demand. In 1804 a new Theatre Royal was built on the other side of town in Beaufort Square. It opened its doors on 12 October 1805 – nine days before the Battle of Trafalgar.

The old theatre became a Catholic chapel and, from 1865 it has been a Masonic Hall. There are guided tours of the atmospheric interior of this fascinating example of Bath's history. The Spiritualist church building on the other side of the street was in Jane's time, the theatre tavern known as the Pineapple.

Paragon [map D2]

The Paragon is one of the main routes out of the city heading north. The elegant terrace of Georgian houses snakes uphill from George Street to merge with the London Road by St Swithin's church at Walcot. The ambitious construction project was completed by local mason Joseph Axford in 1775, the year of Jane Austen's birth. You can see from the aerial photograph that the site is long and narrow and set on a steep slope between two roads.

Jane's uncle James Leigh-Perrot and his wife lived half the year at 1 Paragon, which they rented each winter 'season' from 1797 until 1810 after which time they moved to a house they had purchased in Great Pulteney Street.

Jane stayed with them at 1 Paragon in 1797 when she was almost twenty-two. Soon after this first visit to Bath, Jane was inspired to write *Northanger Abbey* in which her heroine Catherine Morland was all eager delight as they approached the fine and striking environs of the city.

Unfortunately no letters of Jane's survive from this time because, in addition to her mother, she was accompanied by her beloved sister Cassandra, who was her principal correspondent whenever the sisters were separated on family visits.

The following autumn of 1798, Mrs Leigh-Perrot sent a repeat invitation to her Austen relations but Jane was less enthusiastic because she had previously detected a mean side to her aunt's personality. She wrote to Cassandra, who was staying with their brother Edward in Kent, suggesting that their aunt would regret her generosity in inviting them again so soon.

Jane's second visit to Bath was in the summer of 1799. This time she travelled with Edward and members of his family. He was feeling poorly and his doctor had recommended taking the waters at Bath. The much larger party did not stay at the Paragon but rented a house in Queen Square. Naturally, they did call on their relations and found that Mr Leigh-Perrot was also unwell:

'We stopped in Paragon as we came along, but as it was too wet and dirty for us to get out, we could only see Frank, who told us that his master was very indifferent, but had had a better night last night than usual. In Paragon we met Mrs Foley and Mrs Dowdeswell with her yellow shawl airing out... We are exceedingly pleased with the house; the rooms are quite as large as we expected. ... the stairs are so much easier of ascent, or my mother so much stronger than in Paragon as not to regard the double flight... I like our situation very much; it is far more cheerful than Paragon...'

The curving sweep of Paragon runs uphill towards Walcot, linking just over half way up with Axfords Buildings.

Mr and Mrs Leigh-Perrot, Jane's uncle and aunt rented 1 Paragon each season from 1797 until 1810.

Jane stayed at 1 Paragon in 1797 and again in 1801 at the time the Austens were looking for a permanent home in Bath.

In 1801 the Rev'd George Austen gave over his clerical duties to his eldest son James and the family moved from Steventon to settle permanently in Bath. The Leigh-Perrots' house in Paragon became their headquarters whilst they looked for a suitable abode. Cassandra was visiting relatives elsewhere, in consequence there are letters from Jane which discuss in some detail the merits of comparable properties they considered.

Mrs Leigh-Perrot wanted the family to live near her in the adjoining terrace of Axfords Buildings but Jane was not keen: 'We know that Mrs Perrot will want to get us into Axford Buildings, but we all unite in particular dislike of that part of the town, and therefore hope to escape…'

Princes Street [map C4]

Princes Street leads off the south west corner of Queen Square linking it with Beauford Square. Towards the end of his life Rev'd Thomas Leigh, Jane's maternal grandfather, moved to Bath for the sake of his health and lodged in Princes Street with his wife, son James and his two unmarried daughters Jane and Cassandra. The earliest surviving letter from Cassandra Leigh (who became Jane's mother) was written from Princes Street on 12 June 1762 when she was twenty-three. Unfortunately the Bath rate books do not start until two years later so it is not possible to identify the particular house but it would have been only a few steps to Queen Square.

Within two years of moving to Bath, Cassandra Leigh had met the Rev'd George Austen and they were married at Walcot church. This means that during at least part of the time Cassandra lived in Princes Street she was courting Jane's father. From the long, happy marriage that followed we may believe they were in love.

Towards the end of his life the Reverend Thomas Leigh moved to a house in Princes Street with his wife, son James and his two unmarried daughters Jane and Cassandra.

87

Mrs Austen's hopes were set on this corner house. The photograph shows the flank wall. The windows at the front of the house look out over Queen Square.

Perhaps this is the reason why in 1801, when they were looking for a permanent home in Bath, Jane reported: 'I join with you in wishing for the environs of Laura Place, but do not venture to expect it. My mother hankers after the Square dreadfully, and it is but natural to suppose that my uncle will take her part.'

Jane confirmed that Mrs Austen had set her hopes on the house facing Queen Square: '...above all others her wishes are at present fixed on the corner house in Chapel Row, which opens into Prince's Street.'

Pulteney Bridge [map 4E]

Opposite: Robert Adam's design for Pulteney Bridge was inspired by Palladio's unrealised design for the Rialto in Venice. The cost of construction was funded by a loan drawn on William Pulteney's Grenadan sugar plantation.

The first stone in the construction of Pulteney Bridge was laid in 1769 and the project was completed five years later, at the time when Mrs Austen was pregnant with Jane. Pulteney Bridge spans the River Avon and connects the city with the newly built Georgian town of Bathwick. Robert Adam's design for the bridge was inspired by Palladio's unrealised design for the Rialto in Venice. It is one of only four bridges in the world with shops across its full span on both sides.

Jane frequently walked across this bridge to access the city during the years she lived in Sydney Place. In *Northanger Abbey*, Catherine Morland lodges in a hotel in Great Pulteney Street and crosses the bridge on foot, in carriages, gigs, even bouncing happily home one evening in a sedan chair, having attended an assembly in the Lower Rooms.

Within twenty years of its construction, alterations were made that expanded the shops and changed the façades. In 1799 and 1800 floods undermined the central pier causing the north side of the bridge to be demolished and rebuilt in plainer style. During their stay in Bath, the Austens would have witnessed these urgent repairs undertaken by John Pinch, the surveyor to the Pulteney Estate.

Over the next century alterations to the shops included cantilevered extensions on the bridge's north and south faces. In the twentieth century several schemes were carried out to preserve the bridge and partially restore it to the original appearance that Jane would have known.

The building with steps leading down to the river on the south side is now the very popular Riverside Café & Restaurant. It was formerly the Argyle Inn and Tavern, sometimes known as the Argyle Coffee House. Opened in 1791, it was run during the Austen's time by John Gould who had previously sold wines and spirits at 18 Pulteney Bridge.

Trading as the Argyle Inn, it offered good accommodation for gentlemen travellers, including meals and newspapers to read. Today's basement café was in Jane's time the Argyle Tap, where sedan chairmen and servants enjoyed refreshment.

Opposite, clockwise from top left:
Pulteney Bridge in 1804 as Jane would have known it.

A view of the River Avon and Parade Gardens from a shop window on the bridge.

Pulteney is one of only four bridges in the world with shops across its full span on both sides.

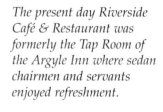

The present day Riverside Café & Restaurant was formerly the Tap Room of the Argyle Inn where sedan chairmen and servants enjoyed refreshment.

Queens Parade [map C4]

Queens Parade is an odd little triangular area just beyond the north-west corner of Queen Square with a terrace of twelve town houses along one side. Number 10 in the row features in the story of the Austen family.

In the 1760s the continuous growth of the upper town as the fashionable quarter of Bath, encouraged some of the leading residents to formulate a proposal for building a suite of assembly rooms here, with coffee rooms and a tavern. Eventually the shareholding investors fell out over the advisability of combining a tavern with an assembly house. In 1768, with the intended scheme abandoned, John Wood the Younger built the terrace of houses seen today.

Number 10 Queens Parade was acquired by William Evelyn who also owned the country estate of St Clere in West Kent. Evelyn was a friend to William Hampson Walter of Tonbridge, half-brother to Rev'd George Austen, Jane's father.

Jane Austen's grandfather, William Austen, married widow Rebecca Hampson, whose late husband had been a member of the Tonbridge-based Walter family. The Walter step-relations were always friendly towards Rev'd George Austen, particularly William Walter who, even after his marriage, kept in touch with Jane's father, despite George being ten years his junior.

Jane and Cassandra also established ongoing correspondence with William Walter's daughter Philadelphia. Rev'd George Austen wrote to his sister-in-law, Mrs Susannah Walter, from Steventon, on 17 December 1775, to announce Jane's birth. He mentions their mutual friend William Evelyn:

'Let my brother know his friend Mr Evelyn is going to treat us to a ploughing match in this neighbourhood on next Tuesday, if the present frost does not continue and prevent it. Kent against Hants for a rump of beef; he sends his own ploughman from St Clair [sic]'.

Jane met William Evelyn in this house at 10 Queens Parade during the summer of 1799, while staying at 13 Queen Square. On 11 June she wrote to Cassandra:

'Edward renewed his acquaintance lately with Mr Evelyn, who lives in the Queen's Parade, and was invited to a family dinner, which I believe at first Elizabeth was rather sorry at his accepting; but yesterday Mrs Evelyn called on us, and her manners were so pleasing that we liked the idea of going very much. The Biggs would call her a nice

William Evelyn's residence at 10 Queens Parade.

woman. But Mr. Evelyn, who was indisposed yesterday, is worse to-day, and we are put off.'

It was the original intention to erect assembly rooms here in Queens Parade.

At first Jane suspected the Evelyns of snubbing them: 'We have not been to any public place lately, nor performed anything out of the common daily routine of 13, Queen Square, Bath. But to-day we were to have dashed away at a very extraordinary rate, by dining out, had it not so happened that we did not go.' Mr Evelyn was finally well enough to receive the Austens for tea and Jane reported: 'the visit was very quiet & uneventful; pleasant enough.'

On 19 June 1799 Jane reports on her brother's state of health: 'Edward has not been well these last two days; his appetite has failed him, and he has complained of sick and

A 'very bewitching Phaeton' like the one owned by Mr Evelyn in which Jane 'had a very pleasant drive' to the top of Kingsdown.

'… a little black kitten runs about the staircase.'

uncomfortable feelings, which, with other symptoms, make us think of the gout; perhaps a fit of it might cure him, but I cannot wish it to begin at Bath.'

This type of comment about gout, 'a fit of it might cure him', also appears in the correspondence of Jane's beloved friend Mrs Lefroy, writing about her husband Rev'd George Lefroy. It refers to the last stages of the condition being the most painful when uric acid crystals are disbursing from the joints.

Regarding Mr Evelyn, Jane continues: 'He (her brother Edward) made an important purchase yesterday: no less so than a pair of coach-horses. His friend Mr Evelyn found them out and recommended them, and if the judgment of a Yahoo can ever be depended on, I suppose it may now, for I believe Mr Evelyn has all his life thought more of horses than of anything else. Their colour is black and their size not large; their price sixty guineas, of which the chair mare was taken as fifteen – but this is of course to be a secret.'

In 1801 when the Austens came to live permanently in Bath they renewed their acquaintance with William Evelyn. On 26 May Jane wrote to Cassandra: 'I assure you in spite of what I might chuse to insinuate in a former letter, that I have seen very little of Mr Evelyn since my coming here; I met him this morning for only the 4th time, & as to my anecdote about Sidney Gardens, I made the most of the story because it came in to advantage, but in fact he only asked me whether I were to be at Sidney Gardens in the evening or not.'

'There is now something like an engagement between us & the Phaeton, which to confess my frailty I have a great desire to go out in;- whether it will come to anything must remain with him. – I really believe he is very harmless; people do not seem afraid of him here, and he gets Groundsel for his birds & all that. – My Aunt will never be easy till she visits them;- she has been repeatedly trying to fancy a necessity for it now on our accounts, but she meets with no encouragement.'

Queen Square [map C4]

Queen Square was one of the first parts of Bath to be developed in the early eighteenth-century by the architect John Wood. It took seven years from 1728 to 1736 to complete and was the initial stage in the creation of the new Upper Town of Bath; the remainder being Gay Street and Kings Circus (now known simply as the Circus).

The initial concept of the square incorporated a unifying façade to the houses creating the impression of one massive mansion on the south side and indeed this terrace did contain a very large house for John Wood himself, which today is the central part of the Francis Hotel. To the right of the hotel, the corner house at number 13 is the one of main interest to us.

Jane stayed here for six weeks in 1799 from 17 May to 27 June. Her brother Edward had taken the house in order that he might 'try the waters' for the benefit of his health, which was considered delicate. In addition to Jane and her brother, the party consisted of Mrs Austen, Edward's wife and their children, Fanny and Edward.

Four letters of Jane's survive, written from 13 Queen Square, during her second stay in Bath. Cassandra had remained at home in Steventon with her father. The Austen family's arrival in Bath was noted in the *Bath Chronicle* for Thursday 23 May. After looking round Jane immediately wrote to Cassandra and it is her letter of 17 May 1799 which provides us with much information about the house.

'We are exceedingly pleased with the house; the rooms are quite as large as we expected. Mrs Bromley is a fat woman in mourning, and a little black kitten runs about the staircase. Elizabeth has the apartment within the drawing-room; she wanted my mother to have it, but as there was no bed in the inner one, and the stairs are so much easier of ascent, or my mother so much stronger than in Paragon as not to regard the double flight, it is settled for us to be above, where we have two very nice-sized rooms, with dirty quilts and everything comfortable.'

Edward Austen took this house at 13 Queen Square for six weeks in 1799 from 17 May to 27 June.

Far left: 'Mrs Bromley is a fat woman in mourning, and a little black kitten runs about the staircase.'

Left: Four letters survive written by Jane from 13 Queen Square.

Opposite, clockwise from top left: *Queen Square was one of the first parts of Bath to be developed in the early eighteenth century by the architect John Wood.*

John Wood retained a very large house for himself, which is today the central part of the Francis Hotel.

The initial concept of the square incorporated a unifying façade to the houses creating the im-pression of one massive mansion.

Jane's view across the square included the central obelisk commemorating Frederick, Prince of Wales father of King George III.

'I have the outward and larger apartment, as I ought to have; which is quite as large as our bedroom at home, and my mother's is not materially less. The beds are both as large as any at Steventon, and I have a very nice chest of drawers and a closet full of shelves – so full indeed that there is nothing else in it, and it should therefore be called a cupboard rather than a closet, I suppose.'

'Elizabeth has just had a very good account of the three little boys. I hope you are very busy and very comfortable. I find no difficulty in closing my eyes. I like our situation very much; it is far more cheerful than Paragon, and the prospect from the drawing-room window, at which I now write, is rather picturesque, as it commands a prospective view of the left side of Brock Street, broken by three Lombardy poplars in the garden of the last house in Queen's Parade.'

It is interesting that Jane mentions the Lombardy poplar trees but seems to have no interest in the splendid architecture of the Square. Her view took in the central obelisk commemorating Frederick, Prince of Wales, King George III's father. In Jane's time the Square was an open paved area but we might presume she would have preferred today's prospect as it is now planted with trees. On the corner, just across the road from the window where she sat, was Wood's Queen Square Chapel. Mentioned by her in a letter two years later, it was subsequently demolished for Victorian road widening.

For Mrs Austen, 'the Square' (so called because it was the first of the important squares to be built in Bath), remained her favourite place to stay.

By the time Jane Austen came to write *Persuasion* in 1815/16, Queen Square was one of the oldest of the new developments. It was far more fashionable to live higher up in the New Town with its crescents and pleasant outlooks across the city and the river. This allowed her a small joke at her mother's expense when the fashionably minded *Musgrove* girls declare that Queen Square is too old fashioned for them to contemplate as a place to stay in Bath for the season: 'I hope we shall be in Bath in the winter; but remember, papa, if we do go, we must be in a good situation: none of your Queen-squares for us!'

The Bath waters certainly did Edward no harm as he lived for a further fifty-three years, dying at Godmersham in December, 1852, at the age of eighty-five.

Rivers Street [map C2]

In *Persuasion*, Rivers Street presents Jane with the perfect geographical and social level to place Lady Russell. The information that Lady Russell's lodgings are in Rivers Street comes at the end of the following evocative description of her impression on re-visiting the city:

'Everybody has their taste in noises as well as in other matters; and sounds are quite innoxious, or most distressing, by their sort rather than their quantity. When Lady Russell, not long afterwards, was entering Bath on a wet afternoon, and driving through the long course of streets from the Old Bridge to Camden Place, amidst the dash of other carriages, the heavy rumble of carts and drays, the bawling of newsmen, muffin-men, and milk-men, and the ceaseless clink of pattens, she made no complaint. No, these were noises which belonged to the winter pleasures: her spirits rose under their influence; and like Mrs Musgrove, she was feeling, though not saying, that after being long in the country, nothing could be so good for her as a little quiet cheerfulness.'

Amanda Root as Anne Elliot and Susan Fleetwood as Lady Russell in the 1995 film adaptation of Persuasion.

Jane's heroine, Anne Elliot gives an alternative impression possibly reflecting Jane's own sentiments, having been forced to leave country life for a future in the city: 'Anne did not share these feelings. She persisted in a very determined, though very silent disinclination for Bath; caught the first dim view of the extensive buildings, smoking in rain, without any wish of seeing them better; felt their progress through the streets to be, however disagreeable, yet too rapid; for who would be glad to see her when she arrived? And looked back with fond regret to the bustles of Uppercross and the seclusion of Kellynch.'

At their journey's end we learn that, Anne was put down in Camden Place, and Lady Russell then drove to her solitary but elegant lodgings in Rivers Street. Situated on the rising ground north of the city centre, Rivers Street is at a higher elevation than Gay Street (where the Crofts had placed themselves perfectly to Sir Walter's satisfaction) but lower than Camden Place where Sir Walter himself and the Elliot family reside.

The location of Lady Russell's lodgings is 'high' enough to be suitable for 'the widow of only a knight' who has a healthy respect for Sir Walter's rank of baronet. Sir Walter would not have condoned her occupying a 'higher' spot on the map than himself but this is a perfect compromise.

Opposite: The undistinguished terraced houses along Rivers Street.

It is interesting that Rivers Street is a fairly narrow road of undistinguished terraced houses. The exception is the elegant house with a three-sided bay, dominating the junction with the wider and grander Russell Street. As it also enjoys an uninterrupted view of the

Assembly Rooms below, can we be in little doubt that this is the house Jane had in mind for the lodgings of her fine lady?

* * *

One house in Rivers Street features in Jane's own story, this is number 10. On 12 May 1801 Jane was staying with the Leigh-Perrots at 1 Paragon. In a letter to Cassandra, she tells her sister: 'We met not a creature at Mrs Lillingstone's, and yet were not so very stupid, as I expected, which I attribute to my wearing my new bonnet and being in good looks.'

It seems likely that Jane and Cassandra had met Mrs Lillingston (Jane spells it with an 'e') on a previous occasion, probably on a visit to Bath, because Jane does not describe her to her sister or mention her as a new acquaintance. At this time Mrs Lillingston was a sixty-year-old widow living alone, except for her little dog, Malore and her faithful maid Molly Stowe, her man servant, Francis Varley and a succession of cooks.

Mrs Lillingston was a member of the Leigh-Perrots' circle of friends. She was born in 1741 as Willielma Joanna Dottin, at Grenada Hall, Barbados, of a long-standing slave-owning and slave-trading family dating from the early seventeenth-century. Also born in Barbados and three years younger, Mrs Leigh-Perrot, was the daughter of Robert Cholmeley who owned land on the island.

10 Rivers Street where Jane visited Mrs Lillingston in May 1801.

One of Mrs Lillingston's ancestors, William Dottin, was registered in June 1680 as 'holding three manservants and 60 Negroes'. The family vessel, the *Dottin Galley*, made many 'double voyages' to the Guinea Coast with a cargo of rum, to return with a cargo of slaves.

Jane visited number 10 again a week later, as she tells Cassandra: 'My evening visit was by no means disagreeable. Mrs Lillingstone came to engage Mrs Holder's conversation and Miss Holder and I adjourned after tea to the inner drawing room to look over Prints and talk pathetically.'

Mrs Lillingston was also in attendance at a small party in Paragon on 21 May: 'Were to have a tiny party here tonight; I hate tiny parties-they force one into constant exertion – Miss Edwards and her father, Mrs Busby and her nephew, Mr Maitland and Mrs Lillingstone are to be the whole.'

Mrs Lillingston was born in Barbados and came from a long-standing slave-owning family.

Poor Mrs Lillingston had prolonged legal disputes with her nearest relations regarding the terms of her late husband's estate. After all the trials with her family, she made her

This fine house, with a three-sided bay, stands at the junction of Rivers Street, commanding a view directly down Russell Street to the Upper Rooms.

own will cutting them out completely and appointed Mr Leigh-Perrot to be her chief executor. Following her death on 30 January 1806 she was buried at Charlcombe, a small village just north of Bath. The elderly lady had developed a fondness for Jane and her sister Cassandra and left them each £50 in her will. Jane spent some of the money on a pianoforte when she moved to Chawton.

The Royal Crescent in 1777.

Charles Brock's illustration of Catherine Morland *and* Isabella Thorpe *who once again tasted sweet fruits of friendship as they walked arm-in-arm in* The Royal Crescent.

Opposite: Jane Cooper *and her family lived here for a while in number 12.*

Royal Crescent [map B2]

The Royal Crescent is the great show piece of Bath. This masterful architectural achievement was begun in 1767 and completed in 1775, the year of Jane Austen's birth. The work of John Wood the Younger, the Royal Crescent is perhaps the most beautiful terrace of houses in Europe.

Mrs Austen's sister, Jane married Dr Cooper and they were some of the early residents to move in to the new houses. They lived for a while in number 12 and then, around 1780, moved to 14 Bennett Street, opposite the Upper Rooms right at the very centre of social life in the city.

After this time, the thirty grand dwellings soon became the residence of first choice for royalty and the upper echelons of society. As such they do not feature in Jane's novels or her letters. However, she does feature the wide pavements and the green slopes below the

Crescent, because they were a favourite place for social walking being part of the Upper Town with an open prospect to the front and wonderful views across the city.

The lack of building immediately in front of the Crescent was due to the restrictions imposed in the original leases for the site. It was then, and still is, a pleasant place to promenade. Jane makes many references to the custom of walking here on Sundays after church, both in her letters and in *Northanger Abbey* when Catherine Morland and Isabella Thorpe head for the Crescent in pursuit of fresh air and better company:

'As soon as divine service was over, the Thorpes and Allens eagerly joined each other; and after staying long enough in the pump-room to discover that the crowd was insupportable, and that there was not a genteel face to be seen, which everybody discovers every Sunday throughout the season, they hastened away to the Crescent, to breathe the fresh air of better company. Here Catherine and Isabella, arm in arm, again tasted the sweets of friendship in an unreserved conversation; they talked much, and with much enjoyment; but again was Catherine disappointed in her hope of reseeing her partner.'

The Royal Victoria Park adjacent to the Royal Crescent is the largest park in Bath. In Jane's time it was known as 'Crescent Fields', but renamed 'Royal Victoria Park' following Queen Victoria's visit in 1830. On the evening of 12 May 1801 Jane could be seen walking here as she tells Cassandra: 'On Sunday we went to church twice, & after evening service walked a little in the Crescent fields, but found it too cold to stay long.'

One of the rooms on show at 1 Royal Crescent.

Number 1 Royal Crescent is a restored Georgian town house, open to the public.

Jane used to walk in Crescent Fields after church on Sunday.

Four years later, on 8 April, writing from 25 Gay Street, Jane reported it being too hot for walking in the Crescent: 'We did not walk long in the Crescent yesterday. It was hot and not crowded enough; so we went into the field, and passed close by S.T. and Miss S.'

Jane's letter was to Martha Lloyd, living with her mother in Ibthorpe: 'Here is a day for you. Did Bath or Ibthorp ever see such an 8th of April? It is March and April together; the glare of the one and the warmth of the other. We do nothing but walk about. As far as your means will admit, I hope you profit by such weather too. I dare say you are already the better for change of place.'

'We were out again last night. Miss Irvine invited us, when I met her in the Crescent, to drink tea with them, but I rather declined it, having no idea that my mother would be disposed for another evening visit there so soon; but when I gave her the message, I

The Duke of York lived at 16 Royal Crescent. The house with the magnolia grandiflora outside is now the Royal Crescent Hotel.

The entrance hall of the Royal Crescent Hotel.

found her very well inclined to go; and accordingly, on leaving Chapel, we walked to Lansdown.'

* * *

Number 1 Royal Crescent is a restored Georgian town house, open to the public. It was the first of the Royal Crescent town houses built as part of John Wood the Younger's ambitious scheme. In the neoclassical Palladian style it represents one of the high-points of eighteenth century urban architecture. The opulent rooms feature authentic Georgian decor including furniture, carpets, and artwork. Among those on view are the dining room, laid for an elegant meal, the gentleman's study, drawing room, bedroom, and a busy Georgian kitchen.

The elegant centrally situated house at 16 Royal Crescent, with a coach house and stabling for sixteen horses, was home to the Duke of York, King George III's second son, who was a contemporary of Jane's. This house is now the Royal Crescent Hotel and the stables have been converted into a restaurant at the rear of the house.

Sawclose [map C5]

Sawclose is a southern continuation of Barton Street leading down from Queen Square. This is the location of the resplendent Theatre Royal. In Jane's time its front elevation and main entrance were around the corner in Beauford Square. It was here, in *Persuasion*, that Charles Musgrove came to purchase tickets from the box office:

'Well, mother, I have done something for you that you will like. I have been to the theatre, and secured a box for to-morrow night. A'n't I a good boy? I know you love a play; and there is room for us all. It holds nine. I have engaged Captain Wentworth. Anne will not be sorry to join us, I am sure. We all like a play. Have not I done well, mother?' Charles was persuaded by his mother to change the tickets for the following Tuesday by which time Anne and Captain Wentworth had the good fortune to become reunited in love and understanding.

When Jane wrote Charles's little speech, the Old Theatre in Orchard Street had been closed for about a decade and converted into a Catholic church. The foundation stone of the new Theatre Royal was laid in December 1804 and it opened on 12 October 1805, nine days before the Battle of Trafalgar. We have to assume, with Jane's love of theatricals, that she visited the new Theatre Royal at least once during the first season which was her last season in Bath. However, the theatre we see today is not as Jane would have known it. The interior was completely destroyed by fire on 18 April 1862.

Richard 'Beau' Nash, Bath's most famous Master of Ceremonies whom Jane would have known by reputation.

The fine elevation toward Beauford Square, with other walls and staircases which remained structurally sound, were incorporated into the present theatre which re-opened the following year.

*   *   *

Next door, on the Theatre Royal's northern side, is another elegant Georgian building formerly the home of Beau Nash and his mistress Juliana Popjoy and presently part of the Strada Italian restaurant chain.

Richard 'Beau' Nash is the most famous of the characters who assumed the role of Master of Ceremonies at Bath. This was of course a generation or so before Jane was born but she would have been very familiar with the reputation and legacy of this former soldier, lawyer and gambler.

The twenty-eight-year-old Richard Nash arrived in about 1703. By 1706 he had become the city's Master of Ceremonies and within a decade had transformed Bath into the resort of

choice not just for the rich, but for the whole of 'polite society'. He did this by laying down a code of behaviour – his famous 'Rules' which were still in place when Jane visited the city.

Nash's rules encouraged sociability between the growing gentry class and the aristocratic elite, who had traditionally kept themselves apart from the rest of society. He forbade hard drinking and the wearing of swords, which often led to duels. He also set out a common dress code and rules of etiquette which made the less fashionably-minded feel at ease.

Nash's influence was a major factor in the increase of population of Bath rising from 3000 in 1700 to 35,000 a century later when Jane became a resident. These numbers were increased by visitors during the Bath season, which ran from October to early June. Richard 'Beau' Nash died in straitened circumstances in 1762 aged eighty-seven. He was still living in Sawclose where he and Juliana Popjoy had spent the latter part of their lives.

Opposite: In 1862 a fire almost entirely destroyed the original Georgian Theatre Royal.

The Strada Italian Restaurant now occupies the house which was formerly the home of Beau Nash and his mistress Juliana Popjoy.

Stall Street [map D5]

At the time of the medieval walled city, Stall Street was the main north-south thoroughfare. The Bath Improvement Act of 1789 provided for necessary clearances in this older part of town. One of the principal undertakings was to widen and refront Cheap and Stall Streets.

At the western end of the Pump Yard a colonnade gives access to Stall Street. The building rising behind the colonnade, on the western side of the street, is Arlington House, standing on the site formerly occupied by the old White Hart, the principal inn of the city at the time of Jane's first visits.

Towards the very end of *Persuasion*, Captain Harville travelled to Bath on a business visit accompanied by the Musgrove family. The companions put up at the White Hart where their suite of rooms included a 'handsome drawing room' with a view of the Abbey and Pump Yard. Here they entertain friends and a couple of crucial scenes ensued when Anne Elliot visited.

'They found Mrs Musgrove and her daughter within, and by themselves, and Anne had the kindest welcome from each. Henrietta was exactly in that state of recently improved views, of fresh-formed happiness, which made her full of regard and interest for everybody she had ever liked before at all; and Mrs Musgrove's real affection had been won by her usefulness when they were in distress.'

From her vantage point at a window in the suite, Mary Musgrove observed the meeting between the devious Mr William Elliot and the equally scheming Mrs Clay: ".... there is Mrs Clay, I am sure, standing under the colonnade, and a gentleman with her. I saw them turn the corner from Bath Street just now. They seemed deep in talk. Who is it? Come, and tell me. Good heavens! I recollect. It is Mr Elliot himself."' This is confirmation of Mrs Smith's revelation to Anne that these two characters are conspiring together.

It is also in the suite at the White Hart where Captain Wentworth overhears Anne talking to Charles Musgrove about the constancy of women which moves him to write a letter to Anne explaining his own feelings of the enduring love he has for her.

*   *   *

When Lady Bridges, Edward Austen's mother-in-law, came to Bath for her health in September 1813 she was accompanied by her son's family and her unmarried daughter Louisa. The party followed the custom of many well-off visitors by staying at the White Hart until suitable lodgings could be found.

The old inn was demolished in 1867 to make way for the Grand Pump Room Hotel. This was used as offices during the Second World War, and became dilapidated and in its turn also demolished. The present Arlington House with ground floor shops and offices above was built on the site.

Inside the White Hart a couple of crucial scenes ensued when Anne Elliot visited.

Left: Stall Street with Arlington House standing on the site formerly occupied by the White Hart Inn.

Opposite: At the western end of the Pump Yard a colonnade gives access to Stall Street and a view of Arlington House.

111

St James's Square [map B1]

In the spring of 1805 Jane and her mother called on an acquaintance living in this large residential square to the north of the Royal Crescent. She reported in a letter: 'Since I wrote so far, I have walked with my Mother to St James' Square & Paragon; neither family at home. I have also been with the Cookes trying to fix Mary for a walk this afternoon, but as she was on the point of taking a LONG walk with some other Lady, there is little chance of her joining us. I should like to know how far they are going; she invited me to go with them & when I excused myself as rather tired & mentioned my coming from St James' Square, she said "that IS a long walk indeed."'

In 1806 Mrs Austen had hopes of moving to St James' Square and viewed one of the houses.

In 1806 when the Austen ladies were at their lowest ebb after the death of Rev'd Austen and still living in Trim Street, Mrs Austen had hopes of moving to St James' Square and viewed one of the houses. A letter she wrote in April that year conveys her feeling of exasperation:

'I had a letter the other day from Edwd. Cooper, he wrote to congratulate us on Frank's Victory and to invite us to Hamstall in the ensuing Summer, which invitation we seem disposed to accept…we are disappointed of the lodgings in St James's Square, a person is in treaty for the whole House, so of course he will be prefer'd to us who want only a part – We have look'd at some others since but don't quite like the situation – hope a few days hence we shall have more choice as it is supposed many will go from Bath when this gay week is over…'

In Mrs Austen's letter, 'Frank's Victory' refers to the decisive part he played in The Battle of San Domingo, fought on 6 February 1806. This was the last fleet engagement of the war between French and British capital ships in open water. With his prize money Frank was now able to marry and he invited his mother and sisters to share a household with him and his new bride in Southampton. In consequence, Jane, Cassandra and their mother left Bath forever in the summer of 1806.

Sydney Place and Gardens

Almost everyone who moves house faces the same conflict between where they would ideally like to live and what they can realistically afford. Often there is a division of ideas between family members. Just such a situation existed within the Austen family in 1801, when they moved from their home in the Hampshire countryside to look for a permanent residence in Bath. During this time they stayed with the Leigh-Perrots in the Paragon who also volunteered their opinions.

4 Sydney Place where the Austens lived for 3 years from 1801 to September 1804.

Though it was expensive Mr Austen favoured the Bathwick Estate on the eastern side of the river across from the city. Part of his thinking may have been that the development was on level ground, unlike the majority of the new buildings on very steep slopes in the Upper Town.

Although she was concerned about the expense Jane was attracted by the prospect. In a letter to Cassandra written on 21 January 1801 she writes: 'It would be very pleasant to be near Sydney Gardens! We might go into the labyrinth every day.' After weeks of tedious searching an advertisement in the *Bath Chronicle* dated 28 May 1801 caught their eye:

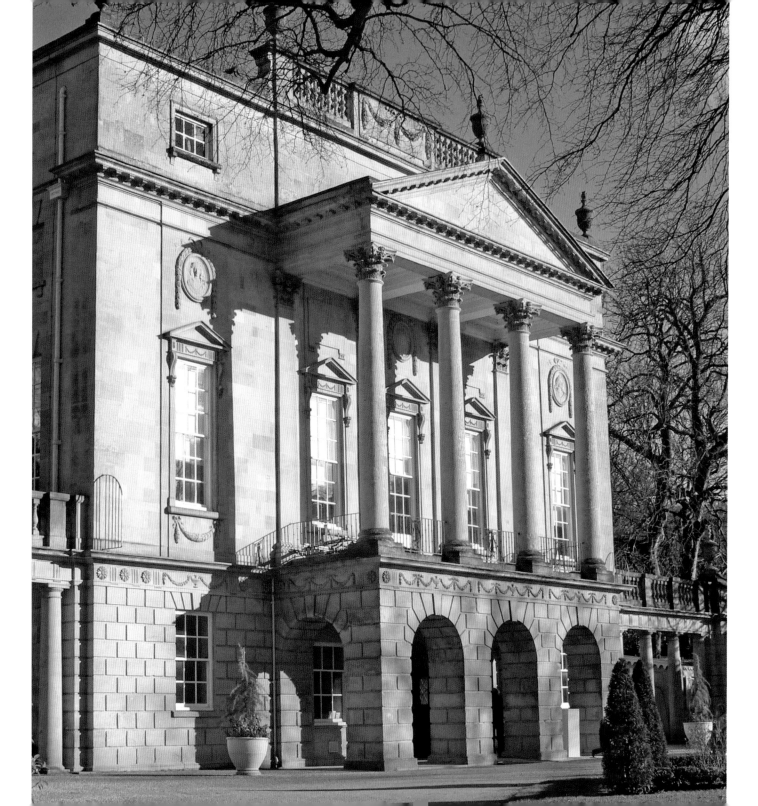

TO BE DISPOSED OF, THE LEASE OF No 4 SYDNEY PLACE three years and a quarter of which are unexpired at Midsummer. The situation is desirable, the rent very low and the landlord is bound by covenant to paint the two first floors this summer – a premium will therefore be expected. For Particulars apply to Messrs. Watts and Forth in Cornwall-Buildings, Bath.

Despite the fact the rent took a quarter of Rev'd Austen's £600 annual income they went ahead. Constance Hill, in her book *Jane Austen, Her Homes and Her Friends (1923)* gives a description of the house:

'4 Sydney Place has four storeys plus a basement. The ground floor has an entrance hall and two rooms: the front room would have been the parlour and dining room used for everyday entertainment and the rear room would most likely have been Rev'd Austen's study. On the first floor there is a magnificent drawing room covering the full area of the house which looks south over Sydney Gardens; the windows are large and it is a very sunny room.'

'On the second floor there are three bedrooms; the parents would have slept in one and another would have been occupied by the two sisters – they shared a bedroom all their lives. The top floor has another three bedrooms, where the servants would have slept. The kitchen in the basement is reached by stairs from the ground floor. There is a small walled garden in which there would have been an earth closet… there was piped water to the house.'

The Austens remained at number 4 for three years. When the lease came up for renewal in September 1804 they declined to take it up. No doubt the trustees would have required a rise in the rent which would have further stretched Rev'd Austen's limited income. They gave up Sydney Place and moved to a house in Green Park Buildings, in the area they had previously rejected.

* * *

From the house in Sydney Place Jane could see the impressive building that provides the focal point at the far eastern end of Great Pulteney Street. Today it is home to the Holburne Museum. In Jane's time this was a hotel called Sydney House through which visitors had to pass to gain entrance to Sydney Gardens.

Although Jane would be familiar with the façade of the building we see today, she would not recognise the interior. There is no longer a banqueting hall, billiard room or coffee

Opposite: *The Holburne Museum was an Hotel in Jane's time.*

Great Pulteney Street from the Sydney Hotel, 1806.

The back of the Sydney Hotel had a row of dining booths (seen off to the right) and a moveable bandstand which the Georgians referred to as the 'elegant orchestra'.

room where the provincial and London papers were available to read. Gone too is the tavern where sedan chairmen could rest and refresh themselves.

Formerly Bath had only been a winter resort but by 1795, when the pleasure gardens opened, there were sufficient city residents throughout the year to warrant provision of summer entertainment. Sydney Gardens quickly became a popular place to see and be seen. Jane had already visited the gardens before she came to live permanently in Bath as we learn from a letter written to Cassandra on 21 May 1799, while she was staying in Queen Square with her brother Edward and his family:

'There was a very long list of arrivals here in the newspaper yesterday, so that we need not immediately dread absolute solitude; and there is a public breakfast in Sydney Gardens every morning, so that we shall not be wholly starved.'

On 4 June 1799, the annual firework display was planned to celebrate the King's birthday but the weather was so bad it was rescheduled for the 18th when Jane attended. On 19 June she reported: 'Last night we were in Sidney Gardens [*sic*] again as there was a repetition of the Gala which went off so ill on the 4th – We did not go till nine and then were in very good time for the Fire-Works which were really beautiful and surpassing my expectations – the illuminations too were very pretty.'

Although Jane enjoyed the fireworks she was not impressed with the music. A couple of weeks after her first letter she reported: 'There is to be a grand gala on Tuesday evening in Sydney Gardens, a concert, with illuminations and fireworks. To the latter Elizabeth and I look forward with pleasure, and even the concert will have more than its usual charm for me, as the gardens are large enough for me to get pretty well beyond the reach of its sound.'

In Jane's time visitors had to pass through the Sydney Hotel to access the Pleasure Gardens.

The famous labyrinth was twice the size of the one at Hampton Court and led down to a grotto and Merlin's Swing. A contemporary description hints at the difficulty of the maze: '… it might puzzle any cunning person, if left to himself and without a clue, for six hours, to acquire the much wished for spot; and it is rather a difficult task when the explorer of the Labyrinth has the direction pointed out to him from a man stationed in the swing. The ins and outs necessary to be made, it is said, measure half a mile.'

In 1800 the Kennet and Avon Canal was dug through the gardens, in order to connect the River Avon at Bath with the River Kennet at Newbury. This became part of the major waterway connecting Bristol with London. There was great opposition to the idea of routeing the canal through the gardens but Pierce Egan who published his *Walks through Bath* in 1819 approved of the end result and thought it enhanced the charm of the gardens as it was:

In 1800 the Kennet and Avon Canal was cut through the gardens. Despite misgivings the introduction of the waterway enhanced the aspect.

The canals engineer, John Rennie, designed most of the elegant iron bridges seen today in the park.

'sunk low between stone embankments, so invisible from the gardens until the visitor passed over a bridge or came upon a balustrade, when they would be surprised by the winding expanse of water with its overhanging trees and pretty bridges. The foremost bridge in this view was built in the Chinese style. The two iron bridges carried the two footpaths, while the sturdier stone bridges carried the ride round the perimeter of the gardens.' In 1909 the gardens were purchased by the city and a replica of the Temple of Minerva built to commemorate the Bath Historical Pageant.

* * *

Today, the Holburne Museum is home to a beautiful and fascinating art collection with everything from Renaissance treasures to masterpieces by Gainsborough and from fine embroideries to exquisite silver. Entrance is free and a new extension includes a garden café opening onto the park which serves fresh, seasonal lunches, delicious cakes and fair-trade coffee and tea.

Terrace Walk [map E5]

The western end of North Parade overlooks the sunken park of Parade Gardens with its sweep of river frontage. Opposite the busy junction, where North Parade meets Pierrepont Street, was the site of the Lower Assembly Rooms which were opened around 1705. They stood approximately where the fountain on the traffic island stands today. Anstey's *New Bath Guide* tells us:

'There are two sets of Assembly Rooms in this city. The view of the river, valley and adjacent hills, makes this one of the pleasantest morning rooms in the kingdom. There is a publick [sic] breakfast or agreeable morning promenade every Wednesday, at the Lower Rooms, during the season'.

Jane makes no mention of this morning use of the rooms but she does use the building to good effect in *Northanger Abbey* when the master of ceremonies James King introduces Catherine Morland to James Tilney. James King was the real life master of ceremonies here during the 1790s.

'They made their appearance in the Lower Rooms; and here fortune was more favourable to our heroine. The master of the ceremonies introduced to her a very gentlemanlike young man as a partner; his name was Tilney. He seemed to be about four or five and twenty, was rather tall, had a pleasing countenance, a very intelligent and lively eye, and, if not quite handsome, was very near it. His address was good, and Catherine felt herself in high luck.'

The Lower Rooms stood on the triangle formed between Terrace Walk and Grand Parade overlooking Parade Gardens.

When Henry Tilney was 'treating his partner to tea' he laughingly accused her of keeping a journal in which he feared he should make but a poor figure. '"Shall I tell you", he asks, "what you ought to say? I danced with a very agreeable young man introduced by Mr King; had a great deal of conversation with him; seems a most extraordinary genius."'

The Lower Rooms, according to Anstey, had a fabulous ballroom 90 feet in length and 36 feet in breadth with a stucco ceiling and fine views of the river, valley, and adjacent hills. Paintings adorned the walls – most prominent was a portrait of Beau Nash - and the rooms were elegantly furnished with chandeliers and girandoles.

There were two tea rooms plus a 60 foot long card room and an apartment devoted to the games of chess and backgammon. The balls, according to the Guide: 'begin at six o'clock and end at eleven… About nine o'clock the gentlemen treat their partners with tea, and when that is over the company pursue their diversions till the moment comes for closing

The fountain marking the site of the Lower Rooms was moved from the eastern end of Bath Street to provide better access through Stall Street.

This magnificent portrait of Captain Wade by Thomas Gainsborough hangs in the Great Octagon Card Room of the Upper Rooms. At the time Wade was master of ceremonies at both the Lower and Upper Rooms.

the ball. Then the Master of the Ceremonies, entering the ballroom, orders the music to cease, and the ladies thereupon resting themselves till they grow cool, their partners complete the ceremonies of the evening by handing them to the chairs in which they are to be conveyed to their respective lodgings.'

The opening of the grander Upper Rooms, built in the newer more fashionable uptown neighbourhood near the Circus, caused a gradual decline in the popularity of the Lower Rooms, despite a considerable sum having been spent in improving the facilities. The building's future as an assembly house came to an end with a destructive fire on the night of 21 December 1820.

The tavern in the basement of the Lower Rooms had an entrance direct from Parade Gardens now sealed with this white boarding.

The Huntsman pub was built in 1750 as a coffee house and later converted into a shop with accommodation above.

The elegant Georgian entrance to the first floor dining room in the Huntsman.

The last building on the southern end of Terrace Walk, on the opposite side from Parade Gardens, is the Huntsman pub. Built in 1750 as a coffee house and later converted to a shop with accommodation above. Well known to Jane, it is the only surviving example of a stone shop front in Bath. Eldridge Pope, the Dorset brewers, acquired it in 1906 and turned it into a pub.

Trim Street [C4]

The building of Trim Street was begun in 1707 just outside the city wall and running parallel to it. The land belonged to George Trim, a wealthy clothier who was one of the first members of the Bath Corporation to defy the general opposition to extending the city. There was no thought of uniform terracing at this stage and the original eighteen houses varied in date and style.

In January 1801 Jane wrote to Cassandra about her sister's expected 'fearful presentment' of having been reduced to living here. Writing of their mother she says: 'But above all others

The number of artists working in eighteenth-century Bath far exceeded anywhere else in the kingdom save the capital itself. Some properties in Trim Street, with extended north-facing windows, became sought after studios. This lucrative profession prompted Thomas Gainsborough to speak of 'picking pockets in the portrait way'.

Trim Street looking west.

Trim Street looking east. General Wolfe resided in the elegant house on the left just beyond the arch.

The arch in Trim Street gives access to Queen Street.

her wishes are at present fixed on the corner house in Chapel Row… In the meantime she assures you that she will do everything in her power to avoid Trim Street, although you have not expressed the fearful presentiment of it which was rather expected.'

I believe there were several reasons Cassandra was expected to be so against this location. The position was confined in the heart of the town and had no prospects of views to the surrounding countryside. The street is narrow, only 29 feet wide and doesn't admit much light.

The buildings were already nearly a hundred years old when the Austens were discussing the potential of the location. A number of the houses had been adapted to serve as warehouses and workshops. Trim Street businesses in the 1792 *Bath Guide* include: John Brabant's 'Tunbridge* and Toy Warehouse', Champneys 'Upholsterers and Auctioneers', William Driver 'Stay Maker', John Portus 'Carver and Gilder', John Taylor 'Hair Dresser' plus a Ladies Boarding School run by Mary Ewing.

A further disadvantage of living in this centrally situated narrow street would have been the air quality. Chimneys belched forth dark clouds of sooty particles. The Woods advertised their houses on the northern slopes as being healthier because the air was much fresher. In 1763, Gainsborough moved out of his 'house in the smoake' for the cleaner air of Lansdown.

General Wolfe, remembered chiefly for his victory over the French at the Battle of Quebec, lived here at No. 5 in the days when Trim Street was a fashionable address.

We can barely imagine how the centre of the city must have smelt. Horses, with their powerful emissions, were the main form of transport. The White Hart Inn alone had stabling for 300 horses and Trim Street was near the even larger Bear Inn. On top of that there were local slaughterhouses, tallow makers, soap boiling businesses, glue makers, tanners and brewers. Nearly every pub made its own beer in addition to the significant number of large breweries.

Trim Street was not the sort of place to keep up appearances or where you would want to invite genteel friends to take tea. This is why in 1805, when circumstances forced the Austens to take temporary lodgings here, Mrs Austen signed a letter rather despairingly: 'Trim Street still'.

*Tunbridge refers to Tunbridge Ware. This intricate wooden marquetry, usually in the form of boxes, was manufactured in the spa town of Tunbridge Wells in Kent. The boxes were popular souvenirs in the eighteenth century. Both Jane and her sister had early Tunbridge Ware boxes, as did Harriet Smith in *Emma*: 'within abundance of silver paper was a pretty little Tunbridge ware box, which Harriet opened.'

U

Union Passage [map D5]

At the time of Jane's first visits to Bath the principal inn of the city was the Bear. It stood adjacent to Union Passage and the location of the constantly busy inn yard was an obstacle to providing a proper carriage road from the centre through to the top of the town.

In *Northanger Abbey*, Catherine Morland's brother James and Isabella Thorpe's brother John chose to stay in one of the hotels in Bath since they were not travelling as part of a family. The same was true for Anne Elliot's cousin William Elliot. Although Jane doesn't mention an address she provides sufficient clues to ascertain that the gentlemen would have been lodging at the Bear.

We follow Isabella and Catherine from the Abbey Churchyard: 'Half a minute conducted them through the pump-yard to the archway, opposite Union Passage…' Here the volume of traffic prevented them from crossing Cheap Street: 'a street of so impertinent a nature, so unfortunately connected with the great London and Oxford roads, and the principal inn of the city…'

At that moment Isabella recognized two of the horsemen. One was her brother, the other his friend, James, Catherine's brother: '… on catching the young men's eyes, the horse was immediately checked with a violence which almost threw him on his haunches, and the servant having now scampered up, the gentlemen jumped out, and the equipage was delivered to his care.' The servant who 'scampered up' would have been an ostler from the Bear.

Today Union Passage is a delightful little shopping lane with a variety of businesses including cafes, bakeries, currency exchanges, travel agents and retailers of silver, shoes, stationery and men's and women's clothing.

Today Union Passage is a delightful little shopping lane.

Union Street [map D5]

Union Street, now running parallel with Union Passage, didn't exist at the time of Jane's first visit. For centuries this street was the site of the Bear Inn, one of the largest in Bath. It was a massive obstruction blocking access between the Upper Town and the old city. Visitors seeking the shortest route between their lodgings and the Pump Room or baths had to pick their way through the inn yard.

Union Street was laid in 1807 to 'unite' or connect Stall Street in the old town with the new and fashionable Milsom Street.

There was talk for years of demolition and creating a proper thoroughfare but while visitors continued to come nobody bothered to do anything. It was only when the fashionable set started to shun Bath in favour of Brighton that action was taken.

The inn and its outbuildings were demolished in 1806 and Union Street was laid in 1807 to 'unite' or connect Stall Street in the Old Town with the new and fashionable Milsom Street, so forming the main north-south axis in the newer part of town. But it was too late.

Bath's attraction for the smart set continued to decline. By the time Jane came to reside here permanently the demography of the population had shifted in favour of retired admirals and clergymen and their families like the Austens. Public functions at the rooms had also declined in favour of the boring private parties that Jane hated.

In *Persuasion*, Anne, Elizabeth, Mrs Clay and Mr Elliot are in Milsom Street when it begins to rain. The ladies turn into Molland's the pastry cook's for shelter. Anne is distracted by the sight of Captain Wentworth when she finds: 'Mr Elliot (always obliging) just setting off for Union Street on a commission for Mrs Clay.'

Today Union Passage is predominantly home to independent businesses while in the wider Union Street are the recognisable chains of H. Samuel, Next, The Disney Store, Tie Rack and W. H. Smith etc.

Walcot [map D1]

In medieval times Walcot was a hamlet outside the walls of Bath. The first church on this site, built by the Saxons and dedicated to Saint Swithin, was badly damaged by storms in 1739. John Wood, the architect who led the astonishing expansion of Bath in the mid eighteenth century, put forward plans for a replacement, but a design by the then Churchwarden, Robert Smith, was selected instead.

Smith's church was completed in 1742, and here twenty two years later, in 1764, Jane's parents, were married. At the time Cassandra Leigh was a resident of Bath and St

Jane's parents were married in 1764 in what became the only remaining eighteenth-century parish church in the city.

Palmer's new church was consecrated in 1777 but within ten years was extended eastwards by two bays.

Swithin's was her parish church. She would have had mixed emotions on her wedding day since, only three months earlier, almost to the day, her father's funeral service had been conducted in the same church.

Walcot was soon swamped by the rapid growth of Georgian Bath's elegant 'Upper Town', and John Palmer (architect of Lansdown Crescent) was commissioned to build a new larger church.

Palmer's new church was consecrated in 1777, but within ten years it also had become too small, and Palmer had to extend it eastwards by two bays. A classical spire, added in 1790 to the existing tower, completed the church as Jane would have known it. St Swithin's became the parish church of Georgian Bath and today is the only remaining eighteenth-century parish church in the city.

Looking down from the churchyard at the shops of which Jane said: 'My aunt has told me of a very cheap one, near Walcot Church, to which I shall go in quest of something for you.'

On 2 June 1799 when Jane was twenty-four and staying with her aunt and uncle at 1 Paragon she wrote one of her chatty letters to Cassandra which included comments about the latest fashions, particularly hat decoration, and a bargain shop at Walcot:

'Flowers are very much worn, and fruit is still more the thing. Elizabeth has a bunch of strawberries, and I have seen grapes, cherries, plums, and apricots. There are likewise almonds and raisins, French plums, and tamarinds at the grocers', but I have never seen any of them in hats. A plum or greengage would cost three shillings; cherries and grapes about five, I believe, but this is at some of the dearest shops. My aunt has told me of a very cheap one, near Walcot Church, to which I shall go in quest of something for you.'

On Monday 21 January 1805 George Austen died in the house at Green Park East. The following day, Jane wrote to her brother Francis with the sad news and informed him that: 'The Funeral is to be on Saturday, at Walcot Church'. Rev'd George Austen was buried here in the crypt. In 1968 his gravestone was removed and placed above in the little churchyard.

The exterior of the church was cleaned and repaired in the 1990s. Respecting John Palmer's original design, a major restoration of the interior in 2008/9 provided a light, airy space for worship which was linked by a new staircase to the fully redeveloped crypt which today is home to the excellent St Swithin's Café, open five days a week for light lunches and refreshments.

In 1968 the Rev'd George Austen's tombstone was removed from the crypt and placed above in the little churchyard.

Left: *The funeral of Jane's father was held in St Swithin's on Saturday 27 January 1805 when he was buried in the crypt.*

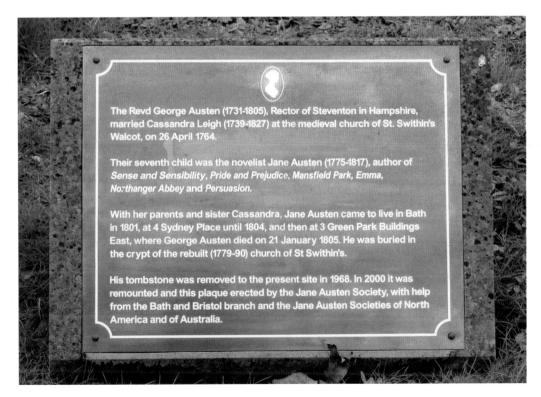

The Revd George Austen (1731-1805), Rector of Steventon in Hampshire, married Cassandra Leigh (1739-1827) at the medieval church of St. Swithin's Walcot, on 26 April 1764.

Their seventh child was the novelist Jane Austen (1775-1817), author of *Sense and Sensibility, Pride and Prejudice, Mansfield Park, Emma, Northanger Abbey* and *Persuasion.*

With her parents and sister Cassandra, Jane Austen came to live in Bath in 1801, at 4 Sydney Place until 1804, and then at 3 Green Park Buildings East, where George Austen died on 21 January 1805. He was buried in the crypt of the rebuilt (1779-90) church of St Swithin's.

His tombstone was removed to the present site in 1968. In 2000 it was remounted and this plaque erected by the Jane Austen Society, with help from the Bath and Bristol branch and the Jane Austen Societies of North America and of Australia.

Westgate Buildings [map C5]

When George Trim breached the old city wall in the north with his Trim Street development, he created a precedent for others to follow. To the west, part of the wall was removed to accommodate Westgate Buildings, putting paid to the open countryside views enjoyed from Chandos Buildings up to that time.

On 3 January 1801, when the Austen's move to Bath was imminent and they were discussing the merits of various locations, Jane wrote to her sister: 'There are three parts of Bath which we have thought of as likely to have houses in them – Westgate Buildings, Charles Street, and some of the short streets leading from Laura Place or Pulteney Street. Westgate Buildings, though quite in the lower part of the town, are not badly situated themselves. The street is broad, and has rather a good appearance.'

A friend of the family was promoting the idea of Westgate Buildings as desirable but we can detect from a letter Jane wrote to her sister on 31 January that Cassandra must have had other ideas: 'Miss Lyford was very pleasant, & gave my mother such an account of the houses in Westgate Buildings, where Mrs. Lyford lodged four years ago, as made her think of a situation there with great pleasure; but your opposition will be without difficulty, decisive'.

Sir Walter Elliot, played by Corin Redgrave in the 1997 film adaptation of Persuasion, *looks with utter contempt on both the names 'Smith' and 'Westgate Buildings'.*

When first opened Westgate Buildings was a fashionable and desirable place to live. However, by the time Jane came to write *Persuasion* the northern slopes of the city had been developed and the fashionable elite were migrating to the lofty terraces and crescents. To Jane's readers at this time, the mention of Westgate Buildings would have conveyed a clear picture of degeneration.

Jane used the location of Westgate Buildings to highlight the snobbery of Sir Walter Elliot when his daughter Anne chose to visit her old friend and former school governess Mrs Smith (née Hamilton) rather than spend time in the upper echelons of the city with her own boorish family. Although only three years her senior Miss Hamilton had shown kindness to the fourteen year old Anne at the time her mother died:

'Her husband had been extravagant; and at his death, about two years before, had left his affairs dreadfully involved. She had had difficulties of every sort to contend with, and in addition to these distresses had been afflicted with a severe rheumatic fever, which, finally settling in her legs, had made her for the present a cripple. She had come to Bath on that account, and was now in lodgings near the hot baths, living in a very humble way, unable even to afford herself the comfort of a servant, and of course almost excluded from society.'

When Sir Walter is confronted by the news of his daughter slumming it in the lower part of town he exclaims: '"Westgate-buildings must have been rather surprised by the appearance of a carriage drawn up near its pavement!"' In fact Anne has the forethought not to embarrass Mrs Smith with the appearance of a carriage and asked Lady Russell to drop her off nearby.

Sir Walter looks with utter contempt on both the names 'Smith' and 'Westgate Buildings'. For him they spell the utmost disgrace: '"Westgate-buildings! . . . and who is Miss Anne Elliot to be visiting in Westgate-buildings? – A Mrs Smith. A widow Mrs Smith. . . . Upon my word, Miss Anne Elliot, you have the most extraordinary taste! Everything that revolts other people, low company, paltry rooms, foul air, disgusting associations are inviting to you."'

'Catherine was so hopeful a scholar that when they gained the top of Beechen Cliff, she voluntarily rejected the whole city of Bath as unworthy to make part of a landscape.'

Walks and Drives Around Bath

Bath is set in classic Cotswold countryside spread across its seven surrounding hills. This enviable prospect provides for many beautiful walks and drives beyond the city. Jane describes taking a carriage drive up to Kingsdown and long walks to the heights of Beechen Cliff and the outlying villages of Charlcombe, Weston, Lyncombe and Widcombe.

Beechen Cliff

A self-declared prodigious walker, Jane used this particular excursion to good effect in *Northanger Abbey*; a novel peopled with energetic young characters eager to explore the countryside around Bath. Catherine Morland and the Tilneys arranged an excursion: 'They determined on walking round Beechen Cliff, that noble hill whose beautiful verdure and hanging coppice render it so striking an object from almost every opening in Bath.'

During the walk there is a debate on the respective merits of novels and historical writing which in turn leads to a discussion on notions of the picturesque, something new to Catherine but very familiar to the well-educated Tilneys. In this passage Jane Austen's irony reaches one of its highest peaks.

Henry's tutelage has a dramatic effect on his young companion who is eager to learn and understand. 'He talked of foregrounds, distances, and second distances – side-screens and perspectives – lights and shades; – and Catherine was so hopeful a scholar that when they gained the top of Beechen Cliff, she voluntarily rejected the whole city of Bath as unworthy to make part of a landscape.'

Jane climbed this 'noble hill' on a fine morning in 1797, proving that she was indeed a prodigious walker.

View of Bath in 1805 surrounded by open country.

We took a charming walk to Charlcombe sweetly situated in a little green Valley.

JANE AUSTEN 2·VI·1799

The residents of Charlcombe are justly proud of their Jane Austen connection.

A view of Bath from Beacon Hill in 1820.

Charlcombe

In a letter of 1799 Jane reported: 'I spent Friday evening with the Mapletons, and was obliged to submit to being pleased in spite of my inclination. We took a very charming walk from six to eight up Beacon Hill, and across some fields, to the village of Charlcombe, which is sweetly situated in a little green valley, as a village with such a name ought to be. Marianne is sensible and intelligent, and even Jane, considering how fair she is, is not unpleasant. We had a Miss North and a Mr Gould of our party; the latter walked home with me after tea. He is a very young man, just entered Oxford, wears spectacles, and has heard that *Evelina* was written by Dr Johnson.'

Adjacent to the churchyard of St Mary's Charlcombe is a 'Quiet Corner' with an ancient 'Holy Well' whose water is famed for being good for the eyes.

The 1000-year-old St Mary's church at Charlcombe is the oldest ecclesiastical building in use in Bath. Inside there is a memorial tablet to Mrs Lillingston.

'*We took a very charming walk from six to eight up Beacon Hill, and across some fields, to the village of Charlcombe.*'

Turnpike Cottage on the Old Bath Road where any coach in which Jane journeyed to or from Steventon, would have halted to pay the toll.

Kingsdown

Jane has written contrasting impressions of Kingsdown, three weeks apart. On Tuesday 5 May 1801 she seems downhearted at the prospect of leaving the country for a home in the city: 'The first view of Bath in fine weather does not answer my expectations; I think I see more distinctly through rain. The sun was got behind everything, and the appearance of the place from the top of Kingsdown was all vapour, shadow, smoke, and confusion.'

By Wednesday 27 May she seems to be making the best of things, riding out in Mr Evelyn's stylish equipage: 'I am just returned from my airing in the very bewitching Phaeton and four for which I was prepared by a note from Mr. E., soon after breakfast. We went to the top of Kingsdown, and had a very pleasant drive.'

On his outing with Jane, Mr Evelyn would have halted his horses at the old Swan Inn which still stands on the summit of Kingsdown.

139

Lyncombe and Widcombe

On Tuesday 26 May 1801 Jane tells Cassandra: 'I walked yesterday morning with Mrs Chamberlayne to Lyncombe and Widcombe, and in the evening I drank tea with the Holders. Mrs Chamberlayne's pace was not quite so magnificent on this second trial as in the first; it was nothing more than I could keep up with, without effort, & for many, many Yards together on a raised narrow footpath I led the way. The Walk was very beautiful as my companion agreed, whenever I made the observation.'

Lyncombe Vale, less than a mile from Bath, developed into a well-known beauty spot and refuge from the city after a mineral spring was discovered there in 1737.

Apart from the farm the oldest surviving building is Lyncombe Hall which can be glimpsed through the trees on the rising ground to the right.

'...for many, many Yards together on a raised narrow footpath I led the way.' The millstream can be seen to the right of the picture.

Lyncombe House was erected following the discovery of the chalybeate spring. It later became a private house and is now a school.

The millstream at the side of the raised pavement disappears into a culvert by the eighteenth-century Lyncombe Vale Farmhouse.

Weston

Now a north-west suburb of Bath, Weston in Jane's time was a country village. On 21 May 1801 Jane wrote to Cassandra: 'The friendship between Mrs Chamberlayne and me which you predicted has already taken place, for we shake hands whenever we meet. Our grand walk to Weston was again fixed for yesterday, and was accomplished in a very striking manner.'

'It would have amused you to see our progress. We went up by Sion Hill, and returned across the fields. In climbing a hill Mrs Chamberlayne is very capital; I could with difficulty keep pace with her, yet would not flinch for the world. On plain ground I was quite her equal. And so we posted away under a fine hot sun, *she* without any parasol or any shade to her hat, stopping for nothing and crossing the Churchyard at Weston with as much expedition, as if we were afraid of being buried alive.'

The churchyard at Weston where Jane and Mrs Chamberlayne: 'posted away under a fine hot sun'.

141

Trafalgar Road in the heart of old Weston.

Widcombe

There is still a significant Georgian feel about Widcombe with buildings and views that Jane would have known. To the left of the church, from a spot near the churchyard railings, is a panoramic view of Widcombe Manor with ornamental cascade and lake.

Ralph Allen was foremost responsible for supplying the distinctive honey-coloured stone, used to build the Georgian city. In 1727, after making his fortune reforming the postal service in Bath he purchased stone quarries at Combe Down and built a tramway from there down to a wharf on the River Avon at Widcombe.

Prior Park, high in the hills above Widcombe, was built by Ralph Allen to demonstrate to potential customers the fine qualities of Bath Stone. Although this was well before Jane Austen's time she would have been very familiar with Allen's reputation and his country house which is now a school. The surrounding park is now owned by the National Trust.

The statue of the White Hart over the door of this Widcombe pub came from the famous White Hart Inn in Stall Street.

The beautiful views of luxuriant gardens and tree-clad hillsides from Widcombe Terrace are more suggestive of Tuscany than England.

Clockwise from top left: *The Norman church of St Thomas à Becket, built between 1490 and 1498, is situated in one of the most picturesque and peaceful locations in Bath. Widcombe Manor was built in the late seventeenth-century; the magnificent Baroque façade with carved keystones dates from around 1727. This row of cottages along the bottom end of Prior Park Road was built in 1737 by John Wood as housing for Ralph Allen's quarrymen. Widcombe Lodge was once home to Henry Fielding's sister Sarah who wrote* The Governess, *the first children's novel in English.*